H. Armstrong Roberts —Philadelphia, Pennsylvania

MASONS WHO HELPED SHAPE OUR NATION

by

Henry C. Clausen, 33°
Sovereign Grand Commander

THE SUPREME COUNCIL, 33°,
ANCIENT AND ACCEPTED
SCOTTISH RITE OF FREEMASONRY
SOUTHERN JURISDICTION, U.S.A.

1976

i

First Printing July 1976 — 10,000
Second Printing October 1976 — 15,000

Library of Congress Catalog Card Number 76-15904

COVER PHOTO:
H. Armstrong Roberts —Philadelphia, Pennsylvania

DEDICATION

To all those Masons whose
contributions to progress have made
our Nation vital and great.

Henry C. Clausen

HENRY C. CLAUSEN, 33°

Sovereign Grand Commander of The Supreme Council, 33°
(Mother Supreme Council of the World)

Sovereign Grand Inspector General in California

Past Grand Master of Masons in California

PREFACE

Our Supreme Council authorized publication of this volume as a salute from the Scottish Rite Mother Jurisdiction to our Nation's Bicentennial and also to our own 175th anniversary. The annals of the two coincide as my following compilations will set forth.

This book should not merely reside quietly, albeit with dignity and authority, on a library shelf. Instead, it would make me very happy to find this used as a reference book and be "well thumbed." Certainly, it will be an excellent source for talks and additional writings, thus furthering our fundamental purpose. The masterful accomplishments of our Masonic members deserve repetition, again and again.

Sometimes it seems that we of 1976 make history faster than can be recorded. Our patriot founders similarly were more concerned with confronting than with memorializing events. Indeed, many items of Masonic lore already have been sequestered and thus escape description. Hence, all the more reason for preserving and illuminating the available historic accomplishments of our vigorous and gifted members.

History often can itself imbue a sense of drama and often springs to life that which otherwise would be overlooked. I feel that America and Scottish Rite Masonry are entities that belie a basic mathematical axiom, for each is greater than the sum total of its parts. It is therefore hoped that this book, covering a period of 200 years and 175 years, respectively, will present an account that proves somewhat interesting, somewhat sufficient as a chronicle of events, and somewhat adequate and complete as a memorial.

Sovereign Grand Commander

Acknowledgements

A sincere Thank You goes to those who have offered their suggestions towards the preparation of this book. Even though they requested that I make no public acknowledgement of this, I think it would be unfair if I did not mention their names. Therefore, to the following I express my gratitude for their help:

RESEARCH ASSISTANCE: Lt. Col. Dr. John W. Boettjer, The Virginia Military Institute, Lexington, Virginia; Art Brown, Arlington, Virginia; and Aemil Pouler, Managing Editor, *The New Age.*

TRANSPARENCIES: H. Armstrong Roberts, Philadelphia, Pennsylvania; The Metropolitan Museum of Art, New York City, New York; Virginia Museum of Fine Arts, Richmond, Virginia; H. Wallace Reid, Anderson, South Carolina; and Roy E. Dunsmore, San Antonio, Texas.

PHOTOGRAPHS: The Masonic Service Association USA, Silver Spring, Maryland; The White House Historical Association, Washington, D.C.; Kenneth S. Kleinknecht, Houston, Texas; H. Dwight McAlister, Columbia, South Carolina; Victor I. Bull, Charleston, South Carolina; Ford Motor Company, Detroit, Michigan; Girard College, Philadelphia, Pennsylvania; Edward H. Siems, San Francisco, California; the Grand Lodge of Maryland; and National Library of Medicine, Bethesda, Maryland.

PRINTING: Neyenesch Printers, Inc., San Diego, California.

And last but not least a sincere Thank You to those from coast to coast who upon hearing of this undertaking wrote to me with so many helpful ideas.

Henry C. Clausen, 33°
Sovereign Grand Commander

TABLE OF CONTENTS

Let our object be, our country, our whole country, and nothing but our country. And, by the blessing of God, may that country itself become a vast and splendid monument, not of oppression and terror, but of wisdom, of peace and of liberty, upon which the world may gaze with admiration forever.

Daniel Webster

H. Armstrong Roberts—Philadelphia, Pennsylvania

MASONS
WHO HELPED SHAPE
OUR NATION

FREEMASONS AID THE BIRTH AND GROWTH OF AMERICA

Patriotism. Freedom. Achievement. These are the three themes that appear throughout the history of American Freemasonry and unify it as a grand monument built from the labors of dedicated Brethren in every period of our Nation's past. From our earliest history as Colonies, through the heroic period of our fight for freedom and independence, to the Westward Movement, and into the Twentieth Century, Freemasons have made major contributions to the creation, stability and expansion of our Nation, as well as in the areas of industry, science, education and entertainment. There is, in fact, no area of American life that Freemasons have not bettered through their devotion to God, Country and Humanity. It is especially appropriate in this, our Bicentennial Year, that we survey this panorama of Masonic history. The perspective of two centuries of unfaltering development permits us today to realize more fully the scope and depth of the accomplishments of our Masonic Brethren. These motivate us to rededicate ourselves in a continuance of this grand heritage. The pages that follow can sketch only briefly the lives of the outstanding Masons who helped shape our Nation. Thousands of volumes could not encompass all the Brethren who have labored long and well. Nor would libraries of written records do them justice; their truest memorial is America today, for it is they who made our Nation what it is today.

Even before America became a nation in name as well as in fact, numerous Brethren as British colonials were laboring to extend to this new land the doctrines of Freemasonry. Time has blurred the record of this earliest period, and

Major General James Edward Oglethorpe

the services of many dedicated Brothers must go unrecorded but not unnoted.

The lives of two men—James Edward Oglethorpe and Sir William Johnson—are representative of Masonic influence upon the young British colony of America. Oglethorpe, a member of the English Parliament, was concerned with both liberty of conscience and the wretched condition of the poor. He organized nineteen associates in 1732 to petition George III to grant a royal charter making an area named Georgia, in honor of the King, a haven for the oppressed of Britain and Europe. Oglethorpe himself sailed with the first group of settlers, founded Savannah in 1733 and, within a year, in February of 1734, convened the first Masonic Lodge in Georgia. He served as its Worshipful Master until the King recalled him to England in 1743. Undoubtedly, Oglethorpe's humanitarian project was inspired by his Masonic principles, and the example of the Georgia settlement based on brotherhood and freedom was not lost on the American patriots of the Revolution four decades later.

As Oglethorpe represented Masonic activity in the South of the American Colonies, Sir William Johnson reflected Freemasonry in the North. In 1766 he was the charter Master of St. Patrick's Lodge, now No. 4, for which he furnished a chamber in the house he built in Johnstown, New York. The house is now a historical monument and contains some of the original furniture, as well as early records of the Lodge in Johnson's own hand.

Sir William Johnson, born in Ireland, came to the American Colonies as the steward of his uncle, Admiral Sir Peter Warren, who had commercial interests here, but he soon became a pioneer in the development of the Mohawk Valley. He acquired vast tracts of land and encouraged immigrants to pioneer homesteads. As a master farmer himself, he imported prize breeding stock, introduced English hay, and selected better seeds and fruits. Under his beneficial guardianship, the Mohawk Valley farmers were soon prospering. The Colony made him Superintendent of Indian Affairs.

He won from the Iroquois tribes the name, "He Who Never Deceives." A key participant in all state councils, he was also a Major General in the British Army during the French and Indian Wars, winning knighthood for his command at the victory of the Battle of Lake George. Foreseeing and fearful of the coming Revolution, but hopeful for a peaceful settlement, he died in 1774. He passed on his faith in Freemasonry to his eldest son, Sir John Johnson, who became Provincial Grand Master of New York. These epic contributions of Oglethorpe and Johnson to the Colonies symbolize appropriately the unsung deeds of service of the many colonial Freemasons whose names have been lost in the mists of history.

Fortunately, the record of the Revolution is written indelibly on the pages of America's heroic past, and evidence that Freemasons participated in the creation of our country fills thousands of volumes. Isaac Sears, for example, was a member of the Committee of Correspondence which organized protests against the British oppression. He met in 1775 at the Green Dragon Tavern with other outstanding Freemasons, such as Paul Revere, to plan the Boston Tea Party. This was often called the Headquarters of the American Revolution. Like John Hancock, Revere was a member of St. Andrew's Lodge, joining in 1760, becoming its Secretary in 1769 and then Master in 1770. An expert silversmith, Revere created fine jewels and seals for several Masonic Lodges and designed and printed the first Continental bills. But it is through Longfellow's poem of Revere's action as a messenger for the Sons of Liberty and his famous midnight ride to warn of the British raid against Lexington and Concord that we best remember him.

At Lexington and Concord a Mason probably fired "the shot heard round the world," for many of the seventy Minute Men who quickly assembled to face the Redcoats were Brethren. They had forged their dedication to America behind tiled doors. John Stark and Ephraim Kirby, for example, were there, and the latter, at Bunker's Hill, received the first of thirteen wounds he suffered during the Revolution—one for each Colony! Joseph Warren, elected Grand Master of the Massachusetts Grand Lodge in 1769, was less lucky. The Bunker Hill Monument marks where he fell. Brother Israel Putnam, a General who pre-

ferred shirtsleeves to epaulettes, fought next to Brother Warren and continued to fight thereafter. He was the only Major General to serve from start to finish in the Revolution, winning the poet's praise:

> Putnam, scored with ancient scars,
> The living record of his country's wars.

In that same fateful year of 1775, Freemasons on other battlefields also fought to sustain liberty. Dr. Jonas Fay, who was to incorporate the Vermont Medical Society later in 1784, was the surgeon of the party making the surprise attack on Fort Ticonderoga in May 1775. Also, at daybreak on December 31, 1775, Brigadier General Richard Montgomery, a Mason in the traveling Lodge of Unity No. 18 under Irish Registry, was shot while personally leading a party of besieging Continentals through a raging blizzard in an attempt to scale the citadel walls of Quebec and take the city by surprise. Again in 1775, the Continental Congress appointed Samuel Nicholas, member of Lodge No. 13 of Philadelphia, Captain of Marines. These first Marines under his command were a picked corps, skilled in the use of small and large firearms and trained to protect America's ships at sea. Under the strict discipline of Brother Nicholas, they soon demonstrated their ability to fight courageously and effectively under all conditions and in any element. During the winter of 1776-77, for example, they reinforced Washington's little army, helped man the boats that crossed the Delaware River at Trenton, and fought in the Battle of Princeton a week later. The famous Marine motto, *Semper Fidelis,* truly describes the spirit of this Freemason and of the corps he founded.

These events at Lexington, Concord, Boston, Ticonderoga and Quebec formed, of course, the growing crescendo of endeavors for freedom and independence leading to the official Declaration of Independence on July 4,

Minute Man
H. Armstrong Roberts—Philadelphia, Pennsylvania

Capture of Fort Ticonderoga
H. Armstrong Roberts —Philadelphia, Pennsylvania

Scene from the Battle at Lexington
H. Armstrong Roberts —Philadelphia, Pennsylvania

1776. Significantly, a number of the 56 signers of this immortal document were Masons. Benjamin Franklin, one of the first Freemasons on record in Philadelphia and an early Provincial Grand Master, and John Hancock, a Brother Mason since he joined the Merchants Lodge while visiting Quebec in 1760, are among the most noted. Others included Joseph Hewes, William Hooper, Robert Paine, Richard Stockton, George Walton, William Whipple, William Ellery and many more whose records were lost in the devastating wartime struggles of our new Nation.

Clearly, the document that declares our national independence, like the Constitution and Bill of Rights to follow, bears the mark of Freemasonry as surely as it bears the bold handwriting of the Masonic Signers, including that of the most prominent, Brother John Hancock, President of the Continental Congress. His defiant oversize signature was so written that George III could read it without his spectacles! The Declaration set forth the Masonic principles that men "are endowed by their Creator with certain unalienable rights, that among these are life, liberty and the pursuit of happiness." It is only fitting, then, that George Washington, the most famous of the Fraternity's representatives, should defend this historic document which Freemasonry inspired. No man had more fully lived the principles of Freemasonry or contributed more to his Craft and his Nation than this great General and President.

Still extant records show that on November 4, 1752, at the age of twenty, young George Washington entered the Lodge at Fredericksburg, Virginia, now No. 4. He was Passed March 3 and Raised August 4, 1753. Despite his overwhelming obligations as Commander of the American Army and later as President of the United States, Brother Washington was an active member throughout his public life and into his Mount Vernon retirement. In fact, when he took the oath of office as President, George Washington

9

Washington Crossing the Delaware
Courtesy The Metropolitan Museum of Art, New York City, New York

was serving as Worshipful Master of Alexandria Lodge No. 22; Robert Livingston, Grand Master of Masons in New York, administered the oath. General Jacob Morton, Marshall of the Day, and General Morgan Lewis, Washington's personal escort, later would both become Grand Masters of New York. The Holy Bible upon which Washington took his oath was borrowed from St. John's Lodge No. 1, New York City.

Since Washington, thirteen verified Freemasons have served as President; namely, James Monroe, Andrew Jackson, James Polk, James Buchanan, Andrew Johnson, James Garfield, William McKinley, Theodore Roosevelt, William Howard Taft, Warren Harding, Franklin D. Roosevelt, Harry S Truman and Gerald R. Ford.

It is a long way from those uncertain days of the Revolution to America's secure position today as a world power. Yet then as now the Nation depended upon Freemasons. Assisting Washington throughout the Revolutionary campaigns, for example, was Brother Robert Erskine, geographer and Surveyor General to the Army of the United States. A Scotsman who had espoused the American cause, Brother Erskine provided information of inestimable value to General Washington, who used Erskine's maps and technical assistance to plan moves against the British. In addition, 33 generals in Washington's army and six of his aides were Freemasons. Outstanding among these was Henry Knox, who had organized the Boston Grenadier Corps, fought bravely in the Revolution, been appointed in the Continental Congress as Secretary of War, served as one of four men in Washington's Cabinet, and was a prime mover in organizing among Continental officers the Society of the Cincinnati. Significantly, when Washington bade farewell to his officers in Fraunces' Tavern, New York City, upon demobilization in 1783, it

Masonic Signers and Independence Hall
H. Armstrong Roberts —Philadelphia, Pennsylvania

William Whipple

William Ellery

George Walton

Benjamin Franklin

Richard Stockton

John Hancock

Robert Treat Paine

William Hooper

Joseph Hewes

was to Knox that Washington first stepped after his formal remarks, extended his hand, and clasped him in a brotherly embrace.

At sea, as on land, Freemasons fought for freedom. John Paul Jones, a Freemason since 1770, wrote a page in American history in 1778 when, as commander of the *Bon Homme Richard*, he answered the British call for surrender with the ringing words, "I have not yet begun to fight!" He was, also, the first to fly the new American ensign in foreign waters.

These many Masonic military heroes of the Revolution were leaders but there was also a great number of Brethren—humble soldiers, marines and sailors—whose names are now lost to history.

Masonic Brethren fought in the Revolution and a Mason concluded the struggle. Benjamin Franklin, a true Founding Father of America, was our Ambassador to France. It was he who mainly guided the negotiations and determined the beneficial terms of the Treaty of Paris that formally ended the Revolution in 1783. The conduct of our international relations was then given to Brother Robert Livingston, Grand Master in the State of New York, as our first American Secretary of Foreign Affairs.

From 1783 to 1789 when the Constitution was ratified, America, now free, had an even greater challenge to implement and preserve that hard-won freedom. The Nation could either unify as one people or disintegrate into a loose federation of States. It was a critical question, the determination of which would set the pattern for the rest of our history. Once more, Freemasons were in pivotal positions working for a strong, united America.

Second only to Washington and Franklin in this movement were Robert Morris and Alexander Hamilton. Often called "The Banker of the Revolution," Brother Morris, like Hamilton, realized that a national fiscal and economic sys-

Masonic Presidents and The White House
Courtesy The White House Historical Association

Gerald Ford

George Washington

James Monroe

H S Truman

Andrew Jackson

Franklin D. Roosevelt

James K. Polk

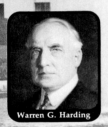
Warren G. Harding

James Buchanan

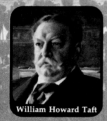
William Howard Taft

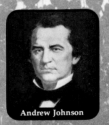
Andrew Johnson

Theodore Roosevelt

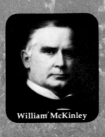
William McKinley

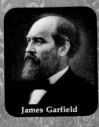
James Garfield

tem was necessary to hold the States together. First steps were made toward this when Morris, who had received a Masonic apron from Washington himself in 1778, was named Superintendent of Finance in 1781 and when the Bank of North America was opened in 1782. Original stockholders were Franklin, Jefferson, Hamilton, Monroe and Jay. The Bank clothed Washington's army and supplied enough confidence in the new Nation to win America international recognition. Hamilton— aide-de-camp to Washington in the Revolution, member of the Continental Congress, and first United States Secretary of the Treasury—supported Morris, proposed extending the Bank into The First Bank of the United States and, with Washington's strong support, succeeded in this endeavor to establish America on a sound monetary basis.

Without the combined financial genius of Brothers Morris and Hamilton, the delegates to the Constitutional Convention in 1787 may not have had the needed confidence to envision the creation of one binding Constitution to govern all the States. On this basis, however, Franklin could argue persuasively the combined political, military, economic and social benefits that the Constitution assured. Brother Robert Morris nominated Washington who was unanimously elected president of the Convention. Thus he gave his tremendous prestige to the constitutional proposal.

The significance of Freemasonry's influence on the Constitution cannot be overstated. Freemasons conceived, argued and ratified the immortal document and, ever since that historic Convention in Independence Hall, Philadelphia, Freemasons have given support to its preservation.

One of the key issues of the Constitution was the creation of the Supreme Court of the United States as the final arbiter in relevant questions. The continuing influence of Freemasonry on the Constitution during this crucial early period was guaranteed when Brother John Marshall was

H. Armstrong Roberts–Philadelphia, Pennsylvania

The United States Supreme Court
H. Armstrong Roberts —Philadelphia, Pennsylvania

appointed Chief Justice of the United States in 1801 and served a record term as Chief Justice from 1801 to his death in 1835. Known universally as "The Father of the Judiciary" and "The Great Expounder of the Constitution," Brother Marshall put his mark indelibly upon all later American history when he asserted the concept of judicial review and enforcement of the Constitution as the absolute law of the land. His lifelong devotion to Freemasonry was central to his thinking and governed his actions as Chief Justice. His own written testimony declares he "became a Freemason while in the Revolutionary Army." He had served as Captain in Colonel Daniel Morgan's regiment, fought at Brandywine, Germantown, Monmouth, Stony Point and Yorktown. He had wintered with Washington at Valley Forge. Like his military and judicial history, his career in

Freemasonry is truly outstanding. He promoted a lottery for the Masonic Hall in Richmond in 1785, where he is listed as a member of Richmond Lodge No. 13, now No. 10. In 1793-95 he was elected Grand Master of Masons in Virginia. Despite all his other activities, he found time to write an authoritative biography of George Washington, fellow Virginian, soldier, statesman and Freemason.

Washington, like other Brethren, felt the new Nation should have a new capital, a Federal City that would symbolize the American spirit, so it was logical that he would recommend another Freemason to help select a site and to design the Executive Mansion for the use of following Presidents. In 1792 President Washington sent Brother James Hoban—later to become first Master of Old Federal Lodge No. 1, Washington, D.C.—to the commissioners of the city and Hoban entered the competition of architects submitting drawings for the President's House. His competition was formidable, for even Thomas Jefferson, an accomplished architect in his own right, submitted drawings. Millions of visitors to Jefferson's exquisite home, Monticello, near Charlottesville, and also to Virginia's State Capitol at Richmond, see proof of the latter's architectural abilities.

Brother Hoban's design for the Presidential House won the day, however, and our second President, John Adams, moved into the Executive Mansion—which a Freemason designed and built. Abigail Adams exclaimed at the time, "This house is built for ages to come." Even the British burning of the Mansion in the War of 1812 caused no permanent damage. Brother Hoban rebuilt the edifice, and he had the exterior walls painted white to hide marks of the restoration. Consequently, the Mansion became known as "The White House," a title that yet another Freemason, President Theodore Roosevelt, formally adopted at the turn of the century.

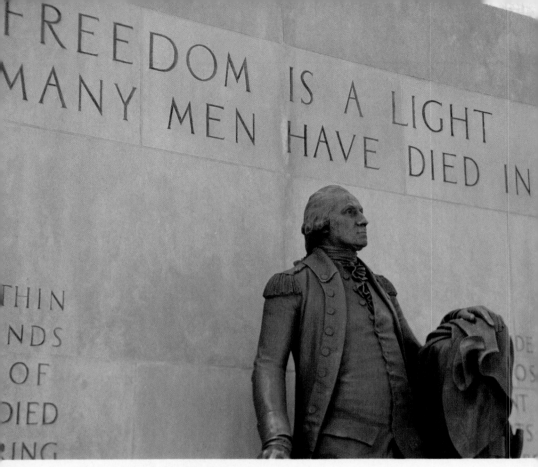

FREEDOM IS A LIGHT
MANY MEN HAVE DIED IN

H. Armstrong Roberts–Philadelphia, Pennsylvania

Under the Constitution and with the guidance of such great men and Freemasons as Washington, Hamilton and Marshall, the States—which Brother Hoban's White House symbolized—unified and prospered. Clearly, here was a new nation based on high principles and eager to make its way in the world. Lack of definite geographical unity, however, hindered this development. Our frontiers blurred into Spanish, French and English territory. It soon became evident to men of foresight that America's manifest destiny was to reach from sea to sea, to combine and include both an Atlantic and a Pacific boundary. Barely twelve years after adoption of the Constitution, Freemasons saw an opportunity to more than double the territory of America.

President Jefferson directed Brother James Monroe, as Minister Plenipotentiary, and Brother Robert Livingston, Minister to France, to open negotiations with Napoleon for the purchase of the Louisiana Territory, a tract of some 828,000 square miles lying between the Mississippi River and the Rocky Mountains. Their quick and clever negotiating closed the treaty of cession for a bargain price of $15 million, less than six cents an acre! The question of the transaction's legality under the Constitution was settled when the Supreme Court, speaking through Brother John Marshall, as Chief Justice of the United States, ruled the Purchase was valid. Moreover, Freemasons not only conceived, negotiated and approved the Louisiana Purchase, but Freemasons Meriwether Lewis, William Clark and Zebulon M. Pike also explored the virgin land.

Brother Lewis, a neighbor of Jefferson at Charlottesville, Virginia, was a member of Door to Virtue Lodge, No. 44, Albemarle County, Virginia. Later, he became charter Master of St. Louis Lodge when it was organized. As Jefferson's private secretary, he managed The White House establishment but he had also both military and wilderness experience as a member of the regular army exploring the Northwest Territory where William Clark was one of his comrades-in-arms at the Battle of Fallen Timbers. Jefferson characterized Lewis as a man "of courage undaunted; possessing a firmness nothing but impossibilities could divert." This presidential estimation was well warranted, and Lewis was the logical choice, with his friend William Clark as mapmaker and artist, to explore the newly acquired territory to confirm America's claim.

The famous Lewis and Clark Expedition set out from St. Louis in May 1804, reached the Pacific Ocean in November 1805, and in September 1806 returned for a hero's welcome

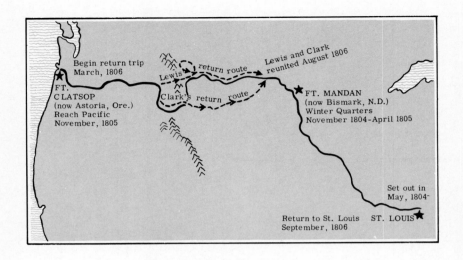

Begin return trip
March, 1806

FT.
CLATSOP
(now Astoria, Ore.)
Reach Pacific
November, 1805

Lewis   return route

Clark's return route

Lewis and Clark
reunited August 1806

FT. MANDAN
(now Bismark, N.D.)
Winter Quarters
November 1804-April 1805

Set out in
May, 1804

Return to St. Louis   ST. LOUIS
September, 1806

in St. Louis. Hostile Indians, treacherous rivers, arid deserts, snow-capped mountains and trackless prairies did not deter these two determined Freemasons. Each step they took established America's claim more firmly. Probably inspired by Lewis's Masonic example, William Clark in 1809 became an Initiate of St. Louis Lodge, of which Lewis was a charter member. Both men, first Lewis and then Clark, administered as Governors the territory they had explored, and together they appointed a secretary, a clerk, a sheriff and four judges—all Freemasons!

Brother Zebulon Pike continued an exploration of this vast area and sought the true source of the Mississippi River in the upper regions of the Purchase. He then led an expedition through what is now Colorado and New Mexico. As a reward for his heroic explorations, he was commissioned a Brigadier General in 1813 but, unfortunately, he was killed defending his country in the extension of the War of 1812.

Like Zebulon Pike, many other Freemasons answered the call to arms in this second war with England, often called "The Second War for Independence." Brother Henry Burbeck, a member of St. John's Lodge in Boston, was, for instance, a Brigadier General and first Chief of the Corp of Engineers. Put in charge of fortifying harbor defenses in New York, New London and Newport, he organized volunteer working parties of the Fraternity to build earthworks with names like Fort Hiram and Fort Masonic. Previously, in 1800, he had recommended the establishment of a military training school for cadets. With the help of two Brethren in high places—Secretary of War Henry Dearborn and Inspector General Thomas H. Cushing—this developed into the United States Military Academy at West Point.

Certainly the most notable of the Masonic heroes of the War of 1812 was Andrew Jackson, the seventh President of the United States and the first Past Grand Master of Masons to occupy The White House. Made a Mason in Harmony Lodge No. 1 at Nashville in 1800, Jackson in 1823-24 sat in the Grand East of Tennessee. While in office, and despite anti-Masonic excitements, he publicly assisted Fredericksburg Lodge at a cornerstone laying of the monument to Mary, the mother of Washington. He is one of the few Presidents to go out of office more popular than when he was elected.

The initial prominence of "Old Hickory" came during the War of 1812 when, in furiously defending New Orleans from an almost overwhelming British attack, Jackson attained a startling victory. The British losses were over 2,000; the American were less than 10. This greatest land victory of the war restored national pride, won Jackson a hero's fame, and elected him to the Presidency in 1828, where he was able to benefit the Nation through acts that his firm Masonic ideals guided.

Unlike Jackson, not all the Brethren were behind guns during the War of 1812. Joel Barlow, of St. John's Lodge

No. 4 in Hartford, Connecticut, for instance, was United States Emissary to France in 1812 and attempted to confer with Napoleon, who was then on his disastrous Russian campaign. Caught in the brutal Siberian winter while on this mission, Brother Barlow died in the line of duty. His loss is all the more tragic in that he was an accomplished poet as well as effective diplomat and brave patriot. His famous "Vision of Columbus," originally written in 1787, was expanded to the final version entitled *The Columbiad* by 1807. In nine books of epic verse, he reviewed the past and forecast the future of a brave new American world. The poem is imbued with Free-masonry and links the great-ness of America to its Masonic heritage.

Stephen Girard
Courtesy Girard College

Brother Stephen Girard, like Barlow, did not fight with military arms in the War of 1812, but without his aid it is doubtful that we would have been victorious. The charter of the Bank of the United States had expired in 1811. Bitter political dis-agreements held up rechartering despite the threat of financial chaos. Brother Girard, perhaps the richest merchant in America at that time, took over the business of the Bank of the United States, restored financial confidence, and, making $5 million available to the government, single-handedly financed 95 percent of the war's cost. Initiated on September 7, 1778 into Royal Arch Lodge No. 3 of Philadelphia, Brother Girard took a lifelong interest in the Craft, served on the board of trustees of the Grand Lodge of Pennsylvania, and subscribed thousands of dollars regu-larly to Masonic projects and charities. Four hundred Masons assembled for his funeral, and eight Past Masters bore his coffin while a Masonic dirge composed especially for the occasion was played. Brother Girard's passing had purpose as well as pomp since he left most of his vast fortune to found Girard College at Philadelpia for poor, male orphans. A Freemason to the last, Brother Girard in his will forbade the teaching of any sect in the school so that students might be free in future life to choose "such active religious tenets as their matured reason may enable them to prefer."

Once victory was won in the War of 1812, America could continue its manifest destiny to expand westward across the continent. Again Freemasons were in the front ranks of those seeking new land and new opportunity for America. Rufus Putnam, designated Surveyor General of the Northwest Territory, was also the first Grand Master of Masons in Ohio and won himself the name of "Father of the Northwest Territory."

Among the famous who were Masons, one must list the first President of the Republic of Texas, Sam Houston. On April 21, 1836, with the cry—"Remember the Alamo!"—(where Brother Colonel William B. Travis had died with Davy Crockett while defending Texas), Sam Houston, as commander of the Texas Army, outwitted and captured Mexican General Santa Anna at the Battle of San Jacinto and so, in effect, won independence for Texas. One year later, in 1837, Brother Houston presided over the Masonic convention at which the Grand Lodge of Texas was organized. He affiliated with Holland Lodge No. 1 of Houston, a metropolis named in his honor. Brother Houston first served as Texas' Territorial Representative and then, after annexation in 1845, as Senator.

Brother Joel Poinsett, the first American Ambassador to Mexico in 1825, who later served as Secretary of War under Van Buren and who strengthened the Military Academy at

Sam Houston

Joel R. Poinsett
Courtesy Carolina Art Association/
Gibbes Art Gallery, Charleston, South Carolina

West Point, is, like Houston, also associated with the Southwest. He is famous because he brought back from Mexico and developed on his South Carolina plantation the plant which was officially named *Poinsettia pulcherrima*. He was a member of Solomon's Lodge No. 1 in Charleston and of many associated bodies in Masonry. It is appropriate that a Freemason should have brought to the United States the poinsettia, a symbol of brotherhood and peace.

In the North as in the South, Freemasons played pivotal roles in adding territory to the Nation. Brother Lewis Cass, Grand Master in two Jurisdictions (Ohio in 1810-13 and Michigan in 1826-28, and again in 1844), had a long and varied career focused on expanding and unifying America. He was Governor of the Michigan Territory, Senator from the State of Michigan, developer of highways and canals in the Great Lakes area, Secretary of War under Jackson, and candidate for President in both the elections of 1844 and 1848. He backed President James K. Polk, a fraternal Brother, in his successful Oregon Purchase and, through some twenty Indian treaties, he added over ten million acres to the national domain.

Fur, timber and iron drew men like Lewis Cass and Governor of New York DeWitt Clinton to the Northwest. Brother DeWitt had already served as United States Senator and Mayor of New York before he founded the Public School Society, which laid the foundation for the public school system in that State. His greatest fame, however, is related to his pioneer efforts to open the West with an elaborate Erie Canal system, completed in 1825. A grand success, it allowed such ambitious men as Brother Alvin Hayward to travel via river and overland routes to the goldfields of California.

Instant wealth in this American El Dorado of California proved illusive for most since to succeed it took hard work, perseverance and courage. In 1853 Brother Alvin Hayward bought an interest in a mine, worked it fruitlessly for four years, and found himself alone when his four partners gave up the project. He had faith, however, and continued under the harshest of conditions until, poverty-striken and at the end of his credit, he struck an immensely rich vein of

The Alamo

27

gold and became the richest man in California. In gratitude to Freemasonry, which had taught him faith in himself and America, he contributed to Sutter Chapter No. 11, R∴A∴M∴ a golden altar and a set of solid gold jewels which are still in use today!

Other prominent Masons also were associated with the California goldrush. One of the first Master Masons to make a permanent residence in California was Abel Stearns, who settled in Los Angeles in 1833 and had the distinction of shipping to the Philadelphia Mint in 1842 the first gold mined in California. Another Freemason, Brother Benjamin D. Wilson, one of the first Initiates of Los Angeles Lodge No. 42, was Mayor of the city in 1851 and pioneered ranching in the area. Brother George Yount also contributed to California's history as the first American settler of the fertile Napa Valley. It was through Freemasons, mainly, that California became a State. Brother Robert Semple, editor of *The Californian*, the first newspaper published in the Golden State, had received his degrees in Kentucky but came to California in 1845 as secretary of the Bear Flag Party seeking statehood for California. He was president of the Constitutional Convention that formed the State's first government and prevailed upon the United States government to accept the former Mexican territory as a sovereign State in 1850. Previously, Commodore John D. Sloat, of St. Andrew's Lodge, No. 3, New York City, as commander of the Pacific Squadron of the U.S. Navy, had raised the American flag at Monterey in taking possession of California. The Grand Lodge of California in 1910 dedicated a monument at the presidio of Monterey to honor this famous Freemason.

The gold fever also had struck Nevada and there, as in California, Freemasons were among the first and most successful miners and organizers. Brothers John Mackay, James Fair, James Flood and William O'Brien formed a lucrative partnership, developed several gold and silver mining properties of the Comstock Lode at Virginia City, and won themselves the title of "The Bonanza Kings." I have written a definitive biography of James Fair's nephew, George Crothers, entitled *Stanford's George Crothers,* that describes this period.

All these Freemasons in the American North, South and West labored to extend our Nation and to enrich it through their hard work.

In the late 1850's America had attained its logical geographical boundaries and was, on a map, one united Nation, but severe internal differences were coming to a head and threatened again to rend the country apart. Northern and Southern factions grew increasingly hostile to each other. Men of good will and peace sought a conciliation and to avoid war. Freemasons above and below the Mason-Dixon Line vigorously opposed the war. In the North, Brother Stephen Douglas, "The Great Compromiser," joined with fellow Freemasons like Southerners John Crittenden and Robert Toombs in an attempt to prevent the conflict and the flow of American blood. In 1861 Grand Master of Missouri, M∴W∴Marcus H. McFarland, voiced the general feeling of Freemasons, saying:

> Our fraternity embraces the whole in bonds of charity. As Masons, we know no North, no South, East or West; yet we know our country and brotherhood everywhere. Peace and harmony are the mission of our Order. Whatever individuals may feel to be their duty as citizens, let us not forget our brotherhood! Let no bitter personal animosities spring up among us! Let us remember the fraternal cord and its duties!
>
> We can do much to assuage the bitterness of the present time by trying "as much as lieth in us to live peaceably with all men," and especially with those of

29

our own household!

May the good God keep you all in harmony and brotherly love!

The fraternal spirit evidenced itself many times during the War Between the States. Masons were known to release prisoners who gave a Masonic sign. Once, for instance, a raid on a home was halted when a woman held up her husband's Masonic apron. Nevertheless, Freemasons on both sides answered the call of their sections and fought bravely for their convictions. Historians have pointed out that the South and North were in spirit, geography, people and custom, separate "nations" dedicated to their respective soils and patriotically fighting to protect their dearly loved independence. The rosters of Union and Confederate Freemasons are long and distinguished. In addition to the more than three hundred generals who were Masons, there were thousands of other Masonic officers and enlisted men. Significantly, the opening hostility of the war involved Freemasons on both sides.

On April 12, 1861 at Charleston, South Carolina, Confederate soldiers under the command of Brother General Pierre Beauregard opened fire on Fort Sumter and, on April 14, Union troops under the command of Brother Major Robert Anderson evacuated the fort. Despite four years of fighting, Brethren like Simon Buckner, Nathan Forrest, Winfield Hancock, Thomas J. "Stonewall" Jackson, George McClellan, John Morgan, Albert Pike, Sterling Price and Lewis Wallace were united as Brothers and all Americans honor their courage and sacrifice. Admiral David Farragut, for example, was one of the great Freemasons who won recognition from all sides for his bravery and patriotism. Made a Mason in a Lodge on the Island of Malta while on duty in the Mediterranean, Admiral Farragut received his greatest fame at the Battle of Mobile Bay.

He lashed himself to the foremast of the steam frigate *The Hartford* and, with the immortal words, "Damn the torpedoes. Full speed ahead!" ordered his helmsman to run the Confederate flotilla. Later in life he revealed that he often said a simple but eloquent prayer that had been inspired by his Masonic background: "O, God, who created man and gave him reason, direct me what to do."

Once the War Between the States was over, Masonic Lodges in the North, East and West sought to alleviate the great need of the Southern Brethren and sent relief funds. The Grand Lodge of Wisconsin, representing the general feeling, recommended that donations be sent "disregarding all questions, differences, and conditions of a civil or political character, and governed only by Masonic obligation." President Lincoln, of course, intended to "bind up the nation's wounds," as he said in his Second Inaugural Address, but his tragic assassination allowed this task to fall to his Vice President, Brother Andrew Johnson. In his attempt to carry out Lincoln's conciliatory reconstruction policy, radicals vilified and almost impeached Andrew Johnson. He held fast to his Masonic principles in the face of terrible opposition, however, and refused to prosecute ex-Confederates. He left The White House under a cloud of criticism, and only today are historians reevaluating the great significance of this Brother who was the 17th President of the United States.

Due to the increase of accurate historical records after the Civil War, our knowledge of the great number of outstanding Freemasons who played decisive roles in the development of America from 1866 to 1976 is so vast that only the very briefest note can be made of a few of these great Brethren in the fields of government and of the military.

Brother William Jennings Bryan, for instance, though never elected President in the three times he was nominated, was, perhaps, the most influential figure throughout the late 19th and early 20th centuries in America. He championed the common man and, in his famous speech at the 1896 presidential convention, expressed his Masonic love of his fellow man in the immortal words, "You shall not press down upon the brow of labor a crown of thorns, you shall not crucify mankind on a cross of gold." Later, as President Woodrow Wilson's Secretary of State, he was able to extend to a worldwide scope his labors for peace and justice.

William McKinley, who defeated Bryan, was, similarly, a Freemason. Under his guidance America became a true world power. He defended the destruction of the battleship *Maine* in the Spanish-American War and signed the bill annexing Hawaii. President Theodore Roosevelt, that famous "Rough Rider" Mason of American destiny, followed McKinley's lead and, through his Corollary to the Monroe Doctrine, established America's special interest in the prosperity and political stability of the Western Hemisphere. William Howard Taft followed "T. R." in this famous succession of Masonic Presidents, and his outstanding achievements were the Interstate Commerce Commission and the creation of the Department of Labor—two moves that formalized the beneficial relationship of management to labor and buttressed the economy of our Nation. After his Presidency, Taft served as Chief Justice of the United States from 1921 to 1930 and continued the great judicial tradition of the fourth Chief Justice and Brother, John Marshall.

"Normalcy and prosperity" were the key words of Brother Warren G. Harding, the 29th occupant of The White House who, despite the ensuing scandals, should be remembered as the central force behind the Washington Naval Conference, which sought peace through a balance of world sea power. Certainly the "New Deal" of Brother Franklin D. Roosevelt and the "Fair Deal" of Brother Harry

S Truman were more than campaign phrases. In fact, they were broad economic and social programs that saw America through the depresssion of the 1930's and the war years of the 1940's. From these two decades there emerged an America of the 1950's which was characterized by the efforts of such men as Brother J. Edgar Hoover, whose *A Study of Communism* in 1962 recognized the essential struggle between the forces of freedom and communistic tyranny and the vital necessity to rededicate America to a defense of liberty, our national heritage.

Today, progress is evident in domestic and international areas, and there is a firm sense of tradition, of building on the fundamental achievements of the past while safeguarding those principles which have made America great.

H. Armstrong Roberts–Philadelphia, Pennsylvania

MILITARY

In the military, as in politics, recent American history has revealed numerous Brethren who have attained positions of great authority due to their lifelong records of patriotic action. It was the perseverance and vision of Brother General John J. Pershing, Commander-in-Chief of the American Expeditionary Force in World War I, that hastily organized American troops were formed into well-integrated combat units which brought victory to America and the Allies. Significantly, General Pershing refused to allow American soldiers to play a merely supportive role and kept them under his personal command. He thereby created a separate *American* force of high morale and efficiency. Brother General George Marshall, a graduate in 1901 of The Virginia Military Institute and aide of General Pershing during World War I, carried the principles of Freemasonry from the battlefield, where he headed the U.S. Army as Chief of Staff from 1939 to 1945, to peacetime when, as President Truman's Secretary of State, he created the European recovery program, the famous Marshall Plan, to reestablish world peace through world prosperity. In recognition of his services, Brother Marshall received the Nobel Peace Prize in 1953.

The highest American military leadership—on land, at sea, and in the air—had a definite Masonic character during World War II. In his autobiography, *A Soldier's Story*, Brother General Omar Bradley notes the deep influence of the Craft on his role as a key figure in the U.S. 1st Army invasion of Normandy in 1944 and on his career as the first permanent chairman of the Joint Chiefs of Staff from 1949 to 1955. Brother General Lyman Lemnitzer, chairman of the Joint Chiefs of Staff and NATO Commander, also is a Freemason and shared with General Jonathan M. Wainwright a Masonic devotion to duty. In command of The Philippines, General Wainwright suffered the tragedies of Bataan and Corregidor as well as the cruel indignities of being a prisoner of war in Manchuria, but he was released in time to be present at the Japanese surrender in Tokyo Bay—a moment of personal triumph for him and a universal triumph for Freedom.

The Allied Supreme Commander who officially accepted the surrender of Japan was, similarly, a Freemason— General of the Army, Douglas MacArthur, 33°. Masonic doctrines formed the guidelines of his outstanding career from honor student at the United States Military Academy, Class of 1903, through his role as Field Marshall of the Philippine Army, to six years as Commander, Occupational Forces in Japan. As a civilian, General MacArthur brought his executive skills to bear as chairman of the board of Remington Rand and then, the Sperry Rand Corporation. Brother MacArthur became a Mason "at sight" in 1936 and affiliated with Manila Lodge No. 1, F∴&A∴M∴. He was honored with the Rank and Decoration of Knight Commander of the Court of Honour in 1937 in Manila and was Coroneted Inspector General Honorary, 33°, in 1947 at the American Embassy, Tokyo, Japan. Brother MacArthur was Crowned an Active Member of the Supreme Council for The Philippines, served as Grand Orator of that Su-

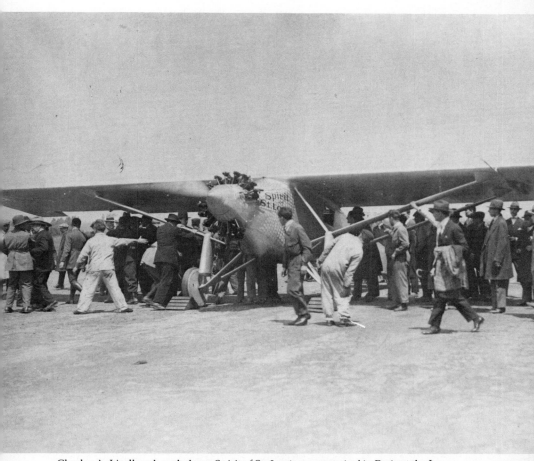

Charles A. Lindbergh and plane, Spirit of St. Louis, upon arrival in Paris at the Le Bourget Field, the landing May 21st, 1927, after solo flight across the Atlantic — *Morton Jacob Traub Jr.*

preme Council for several years and won the Distinguished Achievement Award of the Grand Lodge of New York. Contrary to his own prediction, the memory of this grand "old soldier" and great Freemason will not "fade away" in the hearts of his fellow Americans.

Admiral and Brother Ernest J. King was, like General MacArthur, another outstanding American military figure and Freemason who won fame during World War II. He gained his country's highest honor, the Congressional Medal of Honor, for his bravery at sea. He was Commander-in-Chief of the U.S. Fleet, 1941 to 1945, and directed the daring naval strategy of bringing American ships into Japanese waters. Above Brother King's ships another Freemason, General James H. Doolittle of the Army Air Force, took America's "Crusade for Freedom" into the air and personally commanded the first American bomber raids on Tokyo and other Japanese cities. This brave move revived our Nation's morale during the dark days of the Pacific war and later gave Doolittle the post of head of North African Strategic Air Forces, with which he conducted the massive air attacks that helped bring Nazi Germany to surrender. A member of Hollenbeck Lodge No. 319, Los Angeles, California, and a member of the

Eddie Rickenbacker

38

Scottish Rite Bodies of San Diego, he received the Thirty-third Degree at the House of the Temple in Washington, D.C., in October 1945 together with, among others, President Harry S.Truman, General Henry "Hap" Arnold and Brother James C. Penney.

Another famous Brother, Charles A. Lindbergh, whose epic solo transatlantic flight in 1927 made world history, shared the skies with Brother Doolittle. During World War II, while in his mid-40's, Brother Lindbergh volunteered his services, joined the U.S. Air Force and flew combat missions over the Pacific. Few Americans know the details of his great personal bravery. Most do remember the contributions of Freemasonry to the air war because of the heroic exploits of Brother Eddie Rickenbacker, the leading U.S. air ace, who shot down 26 enemy planes. His rivals that of Audie Murphy, most decorated war hero of World War II and a dedicated Freemason.

The line of Masons—in the Armed Forces—who made substantial contributions to the cause of freedom include among others, Generals—Bruce C. Clarke, Herman Nickerson, Jr., Harold K. Johnson, Willard Pearson, Frederick C. Weyand, Matthew B. Ridgeway, Mark Wayne Clark, Russell P. Hartle, Norman D. Cota, and Archibald W. Lyon; and Admirals—Homer N. Wallin and Joseph L. Howard.

It is clear, therefore, that throughout the growth of our Nation—from founding colonial and revolutionary eras, through the expansion of our boundaries and the desolation of the War Between the States, to the modern century of American prestige and power—Freemasons have played central roles as patriotic men inspired by the doctrines of the Fraternity. As statesmen and soldiers, they have been architects of Freedom, and also have contributed greatly to other fields of American life, especially industry, science, agriculture, education and entertainment.

Cornerstone Laying for the Baltimore and Ohio Railroad
Courtesy M∴W∴ Grand Lodge of Maryland

40

INDUSTRY

In industry, American Freemasons have traditionally upheld the basic economic virtues of hard work, thrift and accomplishment, not as self-serving goals in themselves but as activities intended for the general betterment of humanity. The Founding Fathers of America recognized the essential element of free enterprise in commerce, and such Freemasons as Franklin and Hamilton insisted on a Constitution that recognized economic individualism. Thomas Jefferson, too, said: "Agriculture, Manufacturer, Commerce and Navigation, the four Pillars of our Prosperity, are the most thriving when left to individual Enterprise."

No industry is more representative of this spirit or epic in its dimensions than railroading, and here, as in all aspects of American industry, the influence of Freemasonry is clear. The earliest records reveal Masonic Lodges as part of "cornerstone" ceremonies at the openings of new railway lines. On July 4, 1828, for instance, the Grand Lodge of Maryland assembled in Baltimore to open the Baltimore and Ohio Railroad with proper Masonic ceremonies. The Grand Masters of both Pennsylvania and Virginia were present, and the speaker for the occasion was Charles Carroll, then the only surviving signer of the Declaration of Independence. Similarly, on August 8, 1829 the Grand Master of Maryland, with attending Brethren, opened the Baltimore and Susquehanna Railroad, while the first locomotive of the Union Pacific into Denver is reported to have been decorated with the Masonic symbols of the Bible, Square and Compasses.

The precursor of the railroad in the far West was the famous Pony Express system which developed from a western freight firm, Russell, Majors and Waddell, of which Alexander Majors and William H. Russell were Masons. The joint concern, mainly supported by Masonic shareholders, transported supplies to far western military posts. The efficient and safe conduct of the business gave confidence to many settlers and encouraged them to migrate west along lines established by this firm, thus contributing to the building of the Nation.

By 1860 Brother Majors (a member of Golden Square Lodge No. 107 of Westport, Missouri) and Brother Russell (Initiated in Lafayette Lodge No. 32, Lexington, Missouri, in 1848 and Master in 1852) opened the Pony Express from St. Joseph, Missouri, to Sacramento, California, a journey of nearly two weeks of continuous hard riding, day and night, through territory of every description. Such pioneer ventures opened the way for stagecoaches and, finally, for the railroads. As always, Freemasons were in the front ranks of these patriotic endeavors.

That great moment, for instance, on May 10, 1869 when the Nation was unified by the bands of steel railroad tracks joining the Union Pacific and the Central Pacific Railroads at Promontory Point, Utah, two Freemasons were directly involved. Brother Watson N. Shilling, then Worshipful

Master of Weber Lodge No. 6 and Grand Master of the Grand Lodge of Utah in 1892, was selected for the honor of sending to all the world the news of the driving of the "golden spike." He was the telegraph operator at Ogden, Utah, and had assisted the vital communications needed in building 1,776 miles (a significant number this year!) of track with 20,000 laborers over blistering deserts, rugged mountains and deep ravines. His historic words, "The last rail is laid, the last spike driven," thrilled all America but especially the heart of Leland Stanford, an owner of the Central Pacific Railroad and a member of the Craft. Leland Stanford Lodge No. 784 is named after him, as is Stanford University, which he founded. Brothers Shilling and Stanford had faith in America and united East to West at Promontory Point. Other Freemason railroad builders shared their belief and worked in all sections of the Nation to forge economic bonds of commerce between the States. The Seaboard Railway and the Southern Railway, for instance, honor Colonel A. B. Andrews. He was made a Mason in Clinton Lodge No. 124, Lowsburg, North Carolina, in 1864 where, due to severe wounds, he was on furlough from the Confederate Army. He remained a Freemason for 51 years, superintended the Seaboard Railway and became Vice President of the Southern Railway. In Missouri, Brother Benjamin Grover, like Brother Andrews, helped develop railroad systems uniting the principal cities of his State. Essentially a prosperous merchant, Brother Grover led the reorganization of public schools in Missouri, was elected sheriff, then State Senator, and assisted in the organization of the first Masonic Lodge in Johnson County, Johnson Lodge No. 85. In 1853 he and other Freemasons pressed for and passed a general incorporation act that allowed the construction across Missouri of the Pacific Railroad, the North Missouri, and other railroads, thereby greatly benefitting the growing State of Missouri.

Many patriots contributed to the development of the vast modern communications industry, and, in the 20th century, television owes its popularity in large part to a Brother, David Sarnoff. From humble beginnings in the Marconi Wireless Company, Brother Sarnoff became general manager and, after 1930, president of the Radio Corporation of America. He had the vision to foresee the possibilities of television and played a major role in developing the complex technology associated with the video industry. After serving President Dwight D. Eisenhower as adviser on communications, Brother and General Sarnoff moved to national prominence as a spokesman for the broadcasting industry and for Americanism.

Other Freemasons contributed to America's development through their labors in another great industry—shipping and shipbuilding.

The steamboat's inventor was Brother John Fitch, a member of Bristol Lodge No. 25, Bristol, Pennsylvania, and *not* Robert Fulton. Fitch's first model was built in 1785 and, on August 22, 1787, he made a trial run on the Delaware River at Philadelphia in the presence of members of Congress meeting in convention to frame the Constitution. This was seventeen years before Fulton's first trip. By 1790 Brother Fitch established regular steamboat passenger service, at the speed of eight miles an hour, between Philadelphia and Burlington. The invention was legally patented in 1791 but, unable to win financial support, Brother Fitch left for Europe to seek aid. Ill luck pursued him and he failed. Brother Fitch correctly predicted before his death in 1798, "The day will come when some more powerful man will get fame and riches for *my* invention." He was correct.

Another pioneer nautical inventor and Freemason was Simon Lake, a naval architect, who in 1897 built the *Argonaut*, the first submarine to operate successfully in the open sea. He was Initiated in Monmouth Lodge No. 172,

John Fitch's Steamboat

Atlantic Highlands, New Jersey, and affiliated with Ansantawae Lodge No. 89, Milford, Connecticut, in 1910. In addition to a variety of submarines, Brother Lake developed advanced apparatus for both locating and recovering sunken vessels and for cultivating sponges and pearls. His heavy oil internal combustion engine for marine purposes powered our Nation's Navy and merchant marine. Brother Lake died in 1945 at the age of 79, having devoted a full half-century to making America a world seapower.

Public air service and the commercial airlines industry are also noted for outstanding members of the Craft. Harry S. New, while Postmaster General in 1918, established the Nation's first airmail service. Prior to serving in the Cabinets of both Presidents Harding and Coolidge,

Brother New was United States Senator from Indiana and a leading publisher. In 1933-34 he was the United States Commissioner of the Century of Progress Exposition at Chicago, an appropriate celebration of America's rapid technological and social development. He was a member of Ancient Landmarks Lodge No. 319, Indianapolis.

Brother New's fraternal tie and his interest in aviation were shared with Brother Charles A. Lindbergh. Initiated and Raised by Keystone Lodge No. 243, St. Louis, Missouri, Brother Lindbergh was commissioned in the Air Force Reserve. He became an airmail pilot before winning world acclaim for his solo, nonstop transatlantic flight on May 21, 1927 in the *Spirit of St. Louis* from Roosevelt Field, New Jersey, to Paris. During the flight, Brother Lindbergh wore on his jacket as a goodluck piece the Square and Compasses, and in 1928 he received a gold Certificate of Membership from his Lodge. He became a member of St. Louis Chapter 22 of the National Sojourners. Brother Lindbergh was promoted to colonel after the transatlantic flight and later appointed to the Advisory Committee for Aeronautics, in which position he did much to advance American air development.

Brother Eddie Rickenbacker, the World War I ace of America, was Initiated and Raised in 1922 in Palestine Lodge No. 357, of Detroit, Michigan. When he returned to civilian life, he became connected with the aviation industry, later becoming general manager of Eastern Airlines in 1935 and building it into one of the largest domestic air carriers in the Nation. As president and then chairman of the Board of Eastern, he often spoke out on national issues and won wide public influence as a defender of free enterprise, American air superiority in all fields, and patriotism.

Another World War I ace was Colonel Elliot W. Springs. He was Raised as a Master Mason in 1923 in Catawba Lodge No. 56, Fort Mill, South Carolina. Known for his innovative advertising slogan, "Clothes Make the Man," Brother Springs was the manufacturer of the famous Springmade Sheets and one of the outstanding leaders of the fabric industry in America.

Perhaps the greatest American industrial giant and Freemason of recent years was Henry Ford, a member of Palestine Lodge No. 357, Detroit, Michigan. As a pioneer automobile manufacturer, he introduced assembly line production for a cheap, efficient automobile and mass consumption, thus revolutionizing the American industrial system. Over 15 million Model T Fords were produced, and America became a nation on wheels. Brother Ford's concern for his workers gained national fame in 1914 when he announced a then record wage of $5 for an eight-hour day, in addition to a sophisticated profit-sharing plan that would redistribute company profits to the workers, thereby creating a true people's capitalism. Before World War I, Henry Ford evidenced his firmly held Masonic belief in peace and personally financed a peace delegation to Europe in 1915. Once America's entry into the war was declared in 1917, however, he converted automobile plants to the mass production of ambulances, airplanes, munitions and tanks for the war effort. Similar war material production in World War II won Brother Ford the thanks of a grateful Nation. The Craft is proud to recognize Henry Ford as a Brother and among the foremost giants of American industry who placed patriotism before personal gain and who gave to America and the American People the highest standard of living in the world today.

Henry Ford improved the lot of the urban worker whereas another Freemason, Brother Oliver Hudson Kelley, himself a farmer, took the cause of the agricultural worker to heart and was one of the first farm labor leaders to gain national recognition. From 1849 to 1864 he homesteaded on the Minnesota frontier and witnessed the hard-

Henry Ford and His Early Cars
Courtesy the Ford Motor Company—Detroit, Michigan

ships of rural life. His membership in the Craft, St. Paul
Lodge No. 3, since 1848, gave him the idea of founding a
fraternal organization of agriculturalists which would
unify the American farmer and give him political power.
The preamble to the constitution of Kelley's Patrons of
Husbandry in 1867 reflects Masonic phrasing and influence:

> The ultimate object of this organization is for mutual
> instruction and protection, to lighten labor by
> diffusing a knowledge of its aims and purposes, to
> expand the mind by tracing the beautiful laws the
> Great Creator has established in the Universe, and to
> enlarge our views of creative wisdom and power.

From this concept rooted in Freemasonry there developed the extensive Grange movement of the late 19th century, a movement which still has a deep influence on the American farmer today.

Kelley's organization of the farmer, like the organization of the American factory worker through a fellow Mason, Samuel Gompers, member of Dawson Lodge No. 16, Washington, D.C., avoided radicalism and socialism, stressing instead the basic American Way toward a better life and more freedom for the laborer. Brother Samuel Gompers developed the movement which became the American Federation of Labor in 1886 and which he headed until his death in 1924. During World War I, as head of the Committee on Labor and as a member of the Council on National Defense, he refused to entertain various socialistic regimentations of the American worker. Through his great personal integrity, he held organized labor loyal to government programs, boosted the war effort, and gained general public respect for the labor movement.

Oliver Hudson Kelley

The products of the farmers that Brother Kelley organized and that those workers of Brother Gompers manufactured often were distributed and marketed through the efforts of another outstanding Freemason, the late James C. Penney. Beginning in Kemmerer, Wyoming, in 1902, Brother Penney significantly named his business the "Golden Rule Store." Applying the Masonic lessons he learned from the Craft, Penney and his partners "to the utmost of our ability . . . made the Golden Rule our guide toward one another and toward our customers." Brother Penney's eloquent autobiography, *Fifty Years With the Golden Rule,* details his career as a pioneer in the mass distribution of quality goods at low prices for general benefit to the individual American consumer and to the Nation.

Thomas Cadwalader

SCIENCE

The achievements of American Freemasons in industry are paralleled equally high in the accomplishments of areas of pure and applied sciences—especially medicine, agronomy and exploration. As early as the Revolutionary Era, there are records of a number of outstanding doctors who were loyal patriots and Freemasons.

Brother Thomas Cadwalader, a physician of Philadelphia, is noted for his use of inoculation against smallpox. In 1750 he delivered the first series of medical lectures in Philadelphia, and was one of the original physicians of the Pennsylvania Hospital, as well as one of the first members of the American Philosophical Society. He was a member of St. John's Lodge, or "First" Lodge, and in June 1738 he was chosen Senior Grand Warden.

Joseph Warren

Dr. Benjamin Rush, a member of Congress from Philadelphia and a signer of the Declaration of Independence, accepted in 1777 a commission as surgeon-general, Middle Department, of the Continental Army and served bravely under the battle conditions at Princeton, Brandywine and elsewhere.

Another famous doctor in the Revolution was Brother Joseph Warren. A member of St. Andrew's Lodge, Brother Warren participated in the purchase of the Green Dragon Inn in Boston, changing its name to Freemasons' Hall. Here in 1769 the Grand Lodge of Massachusetts was founded with Warren as Grand Master. As the Revolution developed, Brother Warren in 1774 became a member of the Public Safety Committee and, later, president of Massachusetts' Provincial Congress. As such, he dispatched Paul Revere on his famous midnight ride, and he immediately approved the fortification of Bunker's Hill. Though a Massachusetts major general, Brother Warren waived army rank, fought beside other volunteers and, as Redcoats swarmed over the hilltop, received a bullet in his forehead and several bayonet wounds in his body. His tragic death made him the first Army physician slain, the first major general to be killed in action, and the first Grand Master of a Masonic Jurisdiction to die in the cause of the American struggle for freedom and independence.

Dr. John Gorrie

Other medical Brethren in American history carried on the patriotic and humanitarian dedication of these Revolutionary doctors, heroes and Freemasons. Brother John Gorrie, a member of Franklin Lodge No. 6, Apalachicola, Florida, which he helped charter in 1837, is credited with outstanding work against malaria in western Florida in the 1830's and 1840's. While caring for his patients, Brother Gorrie noted that cooler room temperatures were imperative to control the malarial fever, so he developed a prototype of modern air conditioning that happily resulted in a first—artificially made ice. He suspended from the ceiling of his ward blocks of ice, which had been shipped from New England, and pumped forced air, at many times normal pressure, through tubes and over the pans of ice and water. Gradually, the tubes became blocked with newly formed ice—the first ice ever made mechanically in America. From these makeshift materials and the principles they involved, modern refrigeration and air conditioning developed, thanks to a doctor and Brother who put the principles of Freemasonry to work in a concern for his patients.

Seated, Dr. William Worrall Mayo
(1819-1911) is flanked by his sons,
Dr. Charles Horace Mayo
(1865-1939) and Dr. William
James Mayo (1861-1939).

Rochester's first Masonic Temple
Building which also housed the
medical offices of the Drs. Mayo
from 1901 to 1914.

Photographs Courtesy
Mayo Clinic Archives

Christopher Kit Carson

The great work of the Mayo brothers, Dr. William James Mayo and Charles Horace Mayo, is recognized internationally. They learned much from their father, Brother D. William Worrall Mayo, a member with son Charles of Rochester Lodge No. 21, of Rochester, Minnesota. Originating as an idea of their father, the Mayo Clinic began in the Masonic Temple Building in Rochester. It then expanded into the great medical center it is today. By 1915 The Mayo Foundation for Medical Education and Research was founded as a branch of the graduate school of the University of Minnesota to carry on the humanitarian work of these famous doctors. The medical research the Mayo brothers began and that is now within the Mayo Clinic is part of the Freemasons' exploration on every front.

Christopher "Kit" Carson, the famous frontiersman, scout and Indian fighter was also an explorer of the American West, charting and preparing it for settlement. Brother Carson was a member of Montezuma Lodge No. 109, New Mexico. And farther west, in California, Brother Luther Burbank later explored botanical possibilities of "The Gold Rush State's" ecology. He experimented with thousands of varieties of plants and developed many new types of prunes, plums, raspberries, apples, peaches and nectarines. Besides the Burbank potato, which revolutionized potato agriculture in America, Brother Burbank produced new tomato, corn, squash, pea and asparagus forms with improved taste, nutrition, quantity and hardiness. His spineless cactus provided a new feed for cattle and, most famous of all, his years of cross-pollination experiments with small native daisies resulted in the large, lovely Shasta Daisy, a flower Brother Burbank wished to reflect the white beauty of Mount Shasta of his native northern California. Late in life, after 72 years of cooperating with the Great Architect of the Universe in creating abundance and beauty, Brother Burbank realized that Freemasonry

Luther Burbank

embodied life's highest ideals, and he sought admission to Santa Rosa Lodge. He was Raised in this Lodge on August 13, 1921. His concept of fraternity was so great that he became a member of the University of Masonry, the Scottish Rite. He was Coroneted an Inspector General Honorary of the Thirty-third Degree of the Scottish Rite in 1925. Masonically, his name lives on for, on October 26, 1955, Luther Burbank Lodge No. 752 was chartered in Santa Rosa, where Brother Burbank's home is now designated a Historical Monument.

Exploration—whether of medicine, botany or territory—must take place on the utmost fringes of man's knowledge, and in this modern era Freemasons have led the way to the ultimate reaches of our globe and even outer space. The world's poles, the seas and space itself have been probed by Brethren desiring to bring enlightenment where there is darkness.

Evelyn B. Baldwin, Arctic explorer, carried Masonic flags with him on his expeditions in order to pay honor to the Craft. A member of Adams Lodge No. 63, Oswego, Kansas, he was also a member of New York Scottish Rite. In 1893-94, as a meteorologist, he accompanied Brother Robert E. Peary on the North Greenland expedition, and in later polar expeditions in 1898-99 and 1901-02 he built and named Fort McKinley and discovered and explored Graham Bell Land in the Arctic.

Evelyn B. Baldwin

Admiral Richard E. Byrd surpassed Brother Baldwin's arctic feats. He became a member of Federal Lodge No. 1, Washington, D.C., in 1921 and affiliated with Kane Lodge No. 454, New York City, in 1928. He was also a member of National Sojourner Chapter No. 3 in Washington. Brother Byrd and his pilot, Brother Bernt Balchen, were the first to fly over the North and South Poles, and on each they dropped Masonic flags, Balchen also adding his Shrine fez. Admiral Byrd received the Congressional Medal of Honor for his 1926 North Pole flight and subsequent special Congressional Medals in 1930, 1937 and 1946 for his epochal explorations of both Poles, exploration that helped establish United States claims in Antarctica. In the Antarctic expedition of 1933-35, 60 of the 82 members were Freemasons, and on February 5, 1935 they established First Antarctic Lodge No. 777 of New Zealand Constitution. Due mainly to his explorations in 1933, when he lived for several months alone near the South Pole, and in 1935,

Admiral Richard E. Byrd in flying suit
with the famous sun compass

when he made his fifth expedition, the largest ever, to that area, the United States Navy organized Operation Deep Freeze and added substantial data to our knowledge of the global environment.

Other Freemasons on other frontiers of knowledge matched the patriotic courage of Brothers Baldwin, Balchen and Byrd. American research of the ocean was conducted in 1965 in programs named Sealab I and Sealab II, and it is continuing today. In Sealab I, four aquanauts lived in the waters off Bermuda for eleven days at a depth of 193 feet—a record in world ocean research. In Sealab II, three ten-man teams spent fifteen days each at a depth of 205 feet on an undersea ledge near La Jolla, California. Three of the key men in these experiments are Freemasons—Brother

Aquanauts attach umbilical lines from the support ship to their
Sealab III habitat—
Naval Photographic Center

Cyril J. Tuckerfield, Jr., Senior Chief Engineer, U.S. Navy, member of Somerset Lodge No. 34, A∴F∴&A∴M∴, at Norwich, Connecticut; Brother Lomaye Hurley, Master Diver, U.S. Navy, member of South Gate Lodge No. 182, A∴F∴&A∴M∴, at Portland, Oregon; and Brother Timothy D. Miller, aquanaut in the Naval Underwater Exploration Program, who is also a former DeMolay from a Masonic family and a member of Lincoln Lodge No. 34, F∴&A∴M∴, in Manila, The Philippines.

The final frontier is, of course, outer space, and Freemasons have carried the Craft into the Space Age both in spirit and in fact. The lunar plaque placed on the moon's surface, with its message of "We come in peace for all mankind," reflects Masonry's ideal of universal brotherhood. Astronaut Brother Gordon Cooper, during his historic Gemini V space flight in 1965, carried with him an official Thirty-third Degree Jewel and a Scottish Rite flag. Brother Kenneth S. Kleinknecht, 33°, (brother of our Grand Secretary General) presented these Masonic symbols to The Supreme Council as permanent memorials of this flight. Brother Kleinknecht, as NASA's manager for the Command and Service Modules of the Apollo Spacecraft Program, has made a major contribution to America's success in space. The roster of astronauts includes many Brother Masons such as Edwin E. Aldrin, Jr.; Leroy Gordon Cooper, Jr.; Donn F. Eisele; Walter M. Schirra, Jr.; Thomas P. Stafford; Edgar D. Mitchell; Paul J. Weitz; and James B. Irwin. Virgil I. "Gus" Grissom, who met with a tragic death in a flash fire at Cape Kennedy in 1967, was also a Mason. All these men risked their lives so that America can lead in space exploration and development. The very names of their craft—*Freedom, Liberty Bell, Friendship* and *Faith*—are symbolic of the patriotism of these brave men who carry on the great tradition of Freemasonry—service to humanity through brotherhood and progress.

Courtesy Houston (NASA) Space Center—Kenneth S. Kleinknecht

Paul Joseph Weitz

Edwin E. Aldrin, Jr.

L. Gordon Cooper, Jr.

Thomas P. Stafford

Donn F. Eisele

Walter M. Schirra, Jr.

Virgil I. Grissom

Edgar D. Mitchell

James B. Irwin

EDUCATION

As is clear from this brief historical survey, Freemasons have been leaders in every significant area of American life. In political, military, industrial and scientific fields they have performed great patriotic services and brought the principles of Freemasonry to bear on the Nation's life. In epochal events and in everyday affairs, Brethren have guided America according to Masonic ideals and held fast to the original principles of patriotism, freedom and accomplishment that brought the country from the status of weak colonies to a strong, unified nation, the leader of the modern free world.

Throughout this development, one aspect of our society, however, has received special attention and care of Freemasons, and that is education. The Freemasons who founded America recognized the unique importance of education and established the tradition of Masonic influence on developing a free public school system. The Father of His Country, Brother George Washington, himself, reminded citizens of the new Nation in both his first and last formal pronouncements that education is essential to the permanence of the government they had created. Benjamin Franklin took some practical steps to effect Masonic ideals in education and founded an academy in Philadelphia, an academy that was to grow into the College of Philadelphia and, later, into the University of Pennsylvania. First, he excluded what he termed "polemic disputes" regarding religion and stressed, instead, practical

Brother Edwin E. Aldrin, Jr. on the Moon

63

studies such as navigation, surveying, agriculture, spoken languages of the day, natural history, chemistry, physics, government and history—practical fields of knowledge that would create good citizens who could benefit society. His academy was a step away from the Latin grammar school that stressed outdated classical culture as a social refinement and a step toward the modern American high school of practical studies and good citizenship. Thomas Jefferson, too, warned, "If a nation expects to be ignorant and free in a state of civilization, it expects what never was and never will be."

This essential link between freedom and education is the crux of Freemasonry's traditional support of the free, non-sectarian public school system. As surely as ignorance breeds tyranny, education creates freedom. An informed, thinking citizenry cannot be enslaved or tricked into surrendering vital rights. Indeed, free and universal education is a unique contribution of our American people to the progress of mankind, and Freemasons have been in the forefront of the public school movement in America since the first law of Massachusetts in 1642 that all children be taught to read. The Revolution was, in part, a protest against the discriminatory English schooling system that had been brought to the Colonies and had allowed a perpetuation of the abuses of the British class system. Freemasons then, as now, accepted the truth of the words of John Adams: "The whole people must take upon themselves the education of the whole people and be willing to bear the expense of it."

As early as 1802, when Brother DeWitt Clinton became Mayor of New York City, we see an example of Freemasonry at work to create and support a public school system open to all. Brother Clinton, Raised in Holland Lodge No. 16 (now No. 8) in 1790 and serving as its Master in 1793 and Grand Master of the Lodge of New York from

DeWitt Clinton

1806 to 1819, promoted the establishment of a public school system for the State, was the chief organizer in 1805 of The Public School Society of New York, and founded numerous institutions of literature and art for education of the general public—all this in addition to his pioneer work in the construction of the Erie Canal, whose opening in 1825 created a surge of western expansion! In a message to the New York Legislature, Brother Clinton revealed firm

Masonic principles regarding education: "The first duty of government and the surest evidence of good government is the encouragement of education. A general diffusion of knowledge is a precursor of republican institutions. . . . I consider the system of our common school as the palladium of our freedom."

Grand Commander Albert Pike, 33°, was also a defender of public education. He realized that proper education in the public schools inculcates patriotism and a shared reservoir of cultural beliefs that create a homogenous nation. Citizens, through education, acquire knowledge of their country and of themselves, thus learning to govern themselves wisely and within the guidelines the founders of that society established. Brother Pike used his position after 1833 as editor of the *Arkansas Advocate* to champion the American public school. He said:

> Education is the greatest . . . yea, the only safeguard of liberty . . . Let every child in the land be educated and the trumpet tongue of freedom will find an echo in every heart. . . The land is hungering and thirsting for education . . . it is time for our salvation, and as inheritors of the legacy of freedon, that we are fitting our children to take our places when we are gathered to the dead, to hold as we hold, the reins of [the] self-government, to enjoy as we enjoy, and to support as we support, the blessings of peace, universal freedom, and liberty of conscience.

Such stirring words effectively urged Freemasons throughout the United States to support the public school movement, and the report of the Committee on Foreign Correspondence of the Illinois Grand Lodge, for instance, as reported in their *Proceedings* from 1840 to 1850, notes many contributions through actions and contributions of the Brethren to public school development in Kentucky,

Indiana, Georgia, Iowa, Missouri and Tennessee. A typical quote says: "The Grand Lodge of Kentucky had a very interesting meeting. The brethren there, never wearying of good works, are industriously engaged in establishing a high school." The history of Freemasonry in Texas reveals a representative special interest of the Masonic Brotherhood in establishing a statewide public school system. A group formed the Philosophic Society of Texas, a society modeled on the group Brother Franklin organized in Philadelphia. All the Presidents of the Republic of Texas were represented and all were likewise Masons. In the Texas Declaration of Independence, Brother James A. Collingsworth said: "It is an axiom in political science that unless a people are educated and enlightened, it is idle to expect the continuance of civil liberty, or the capacity of self-government." President Mirabeau B. Lamar, in his first message to the Congress of Texas, agreed with Brother Collingsworth and said: "It is admitted by all that a cultivated mind is a guardian of genius of democracy and while guided and controlled by virtue, the noblest attribute of man." What was true for Texas was true for all States in the United States. Beyond a doubt, Freemasonry, more than any private organization, aided the growth of a free and democratic American public school system.

Brother Charles Albert Adams, 33°, member of the California Orient of the Scottish Rite, while Grand Master of Masons in California, started in 1920 the now nationwide observance of Public Schools Week which grew into other similar observances.

The Supreme Council, 33°, Mother Jurisdiction, states its educational goals that have characterized Freemasonry in America and promoted liberty and justice. They are:

Pride of patriotism, love of flag and country, respect for law and order, loyalty to the principles of

Charles Albert Adams

sovereignty of the people and of citizen control, civil and religious liberty, and free enterprise, as set forth in our Constitution and Bill of Rights;

An enlightened citizenry through the American public schools and for alien adults the inculcation of American principles;

The use of English as the principal language of instruction in the grammar grades of our public schools;

The complete separation of church and state, and opposition to any direct or indirect diversions of public funds to church-related schools or institutions.

These goals clearly summarize the on-going stand of the Scottish Rite, historically, now and for the future. First, the Rite asserts the truth that without patriotic love of country, respect for the law and devotion to the principles set forth in our Constitution, we invite anarchy and the destruction of all we hold dear in America. Patriotism and virtue never become obsolete in the minds and hearts of members of the Scottish Rite. Next, the Rite recognizes that the public school is the only effective tool to combat the terrible effects

CHURCH and STATE

of ignorance, the greatest curse and downfall of a free people. Statements relating to the use of English and instruction in the principles of American institutions are central to the Americanism Programs of The Supreme Council and other patriotic efforts of fellow Brethren to assure that our national heritage of fundamental freedoms is not lost through ignorance or lack of understanding.

The last point—separation of church and state in education, as elsewhere—is a Masonic goal that dates back to the Framers of the Constitution and Bill of Rights. They feared the despotism evident in the long history of church-state conflicts through church-state unions and made sure it would be an American landmark of freedom. Franklin, in his famous *Autobiography*, warned that "explications of the peculiar doctrines of a sect were very dry, uninteresting and unedifying, since not a single moral principle was inculcated or enforc'd, their aim seeming to be rather to make us sectarians than good citizens." Like the other Founding Fathers, Franklin desired complete church-state separation, and this principle was written clearly and explicity into the First Amendment to the Constitution. Freemasons have defended this concept throughout American history. Grand Commander Pike, for instance, asserted that our Masonic goal is "to educate the youth in schools provided by the State, common to all, without distinction of creed or party, not subjected to any sectarian influences . . ."

Brother Theodore Roosevelt, strong exponent of sterling Americanism, said at one time in respect of religion that we must have a "broad tolerance." Surely, we agree. We agree also that parents legally may send their children to religious schools.

Brother Roosevelt also said this on the precise question presented, namely, state aid to parochial schools:

We stand unalterably in favor of the Public School

System in its entirety.

We are against any division of the school fund and against any appropriation of public money for sectarian purposes. We are against any recognition whatever by the State in any shape or form of State aided parochial schools.

Brother Garfield, in a letter accepting the nomination for the presidency, said:

. . . it would be unjust to our people, and dangerous to our institutions, to apply any portion of the revenues of the nation, or of the States, to the support of sectarian schools. The separation of the Church and the State in everything relating to taxation should be absolute. (II The Works of James Abram Garfield, ed. by Hinsdale, 1883, 783.)

Many American Brethren have implemented the Masonic goal and, as individuals, have opposed sectarian intrusions into religious affairs and vice versa. Prominent among these who have fought successfully for the preservation of the great American principle of separation of church and state is Dr. Glenn L. Archer, Executive Director, and Dr. C. Stanley Lowell, Associate Director of the Americans United for Separation of Church and State; both Thirty-third Degree members of the Scottish Rite of Freemasonry. Their contributions with others of their staff have been magnificent and manifold.

These powerful statements are central to Freemasonry and its relation to education today. We dare not risk and neglect the freedoms we have inherited nor the motivations from which they sprang. Liberty is the result of knowledge, and knowledge is the product of education. As a republic, America today depends on each citizen; therefore, we, as Freemasons, must continue the traditional concern of our Fraternity in creating and sustaining a free public school system unfettered through sectarian entanglement. This is the task our forefathers gave us. This is the responsibility our Brothers before us have fulfilled. This is our duty today.

ENTERTAINMENT

"All the world's a stage," a line from Shakespeare's "As You Like It," applies with especial significance to Freemasonry. Thousands of famous entertainers have been Brothers in the Craft. Through the tears and laughter of the theatre, they have proved one of Freemasonry's fundamental principles, the Brotherhood of Man. In seeing others on the stage, we see ourselves and recognize our common bonds to others. All men share in the joy and sorrow, richness and poverty, life and death that the artist depicts. Theatre can exalt man, make him worthy of our attention and show us the goodness that may strive beneath apparent evil, asserting that men are one in spirit and aspiration. It would be impossible to note all the great personalities of the entertainment world who were or are Freemasons, and the mention of a few will have to suffice as representative of the other and very many Brethren who have brought Masonic ideals to the macrocosm of the world through the microcosm of the stage.

In music, the names of three Brethren stand out—John Philip Sousa, George M. Cohan and Irving Berlin. Brother Sousa, apprenticed to the U.S. Marine Band to which his father belonged, grew up amid martial glory and patriotic fervor. He determined to head the Band himself and became its leader in 1880, serving until 1892. His spirited marches such as "Semper Fidelis" and "Stars and Stripes

John Philip Sousa

Forever," to name only two, are immortal memorials to American patriotism. George M. Cohan's foot-tapping songs, such as "Give My Regards to Broadway," "Over There" and "You're a Grand Old Flag," lifted American hearts during the First World War. As late as 1937 Brother Cohan, who had already had a distinguished career on the New York musical stage, won critical and national fame for his serious role as President Franklin D. Roosevelt in the play, "I'd Rather Be Right." Congress, in a special act of May 1940, voted him a gold medal that President Roosevelt presented to Brother Cohan in The White House. A lifelong Mason, having been Raised in 1905 in Pacific

George M. Cohan

Lodge No. 233, New York City, Brother Cohan received his Scottish Rite Thirty-second Degree in 1906. Irving Berlin was a fellow life member of the Craft, musical genius and a member of Munn Lodge No. 190, New York City. He received the Scottish Rite Thirty-second Degree on December 23, 1910. Melodies like "Alexander's Ragtime Band," "Easter Parade" and "White Christmas" will never be forgotten, but Brother Berlin's deep love of country is most evident in his most moving lyric, "God Bless America."

In the field of mass popular entertainment, Brother William Frederick "Wild Bill" Cody's Wild West show, the forerunner of the modern rodeo, has become a legend, but some forget that, as a Pony Express rider as well as scout, he helped open the West to settlement. Also in the West, as Governor of the Territory of New Mexico, Brother and General Lewis Wallace took time to write *Ben Hur: A Tale of Christ*. As a novel, stage play, and then in successive film versions, this epic tale moved millions to consider the message of brotherhood Jesus and Freemasonry taught. Brother Wallace received his degrees in Fountain Lodge No. 60, Covington, Indiana, in 1850 and 1851. The spectacle of "Ben Hur" was not unlike what the Ringling Brothers (also Brothers in Freemasonry) provided in their lavish

Irving Berlin

circus performances involving the great clown, Brother Emmett Kelly, and the famous acrobat, Brother Karl Wallenda, of the "Flying Wallendas." Brother Harry Houdini, with his breathtaking escape stunts and magic tricks, provided more thrills to rapt audiences. In 1926 Brother Houdini revealed the pride in America so evident in his career when he bequeathed to the Library of Congress his entire library on magic, the most extensive and rare collection in the world of books on this subject.

The film industry, of course, is noted for its great number of Freemasons. During the 1920's, for instance, members of Pacific Lodge No. 233 of New York City were in southern California and were impressed in learning of the many Brethren in motion pictures. They suggested organizing a social club and, during its heyday, the resulting "233 Club" had over 1,700 Masons of the motion picture and theatrical industries as its members, including Douglas Fairbanks, Harold and Frank Lloyd, Wallace Berry and Louis B. Mayer. One of the outstanding patriotic activities of the Club was a gigantic "Pageant of Liberty" in the Los Angeles Coliseum on July 5, 1926 before an audience of 65,000 and employing over 2,500 actors and a chorus of 1,200. Brother Tom Mix, astride his horse, "Tony," portrayed Paul Revere, and Brother Hoot Gibson was a Pony Express rider.

The thousands of film artists who played in this pageant owed their employment, in large part, to a fellow Mason, actor and inventor, James E. Blackstone, who patented in 1892 and 1894 the first practical moving picture cameras. Brother Blackstone held many Masonic offices during his life and received the Thirty-second Scottish Rite Degree in 1901 in the Valley of Jersey City. George Brent, Eddie Cantor, Joe E. Brown, Charles Coburn, Dan Defore, Gene Autry, Will Rogers, Roy Disney (president of Disney Studios and brother of Walt, who was a DeMolay as a

Jack L. Warner

youth), Cecil B. DeMille, Ernest Borgnine and Red Skelton are only a few of the stars of the silver screen, radio and television who have been or are Freemasons and have found in the Craft principles that parallel the deep humanity of their theatrical profession. For more than half a century, Brother Jack L. Warner, 33°, has been a creative force in the American motion picture industry. His name has become synonymous with film excellence, and he has produced hundreds of the finest cinematic dramas and comedies that came out of Hollywood.

Similarly, in sports as in the performing arts, Masonry is well represented. James Naismith, the inventor of basketball, was Past Master of Lawrence, Kansas, Lodge No. 6. In 1972 there were 63 Freemasons prominent in American basketball, including Arnold "Red" Auerbach, who won eight straight world championships for the Boston Celtics,

James Naismith

and was NBA Coach of the Year in 1965. Fraternal foot-
ballers of prominence numbered nearly three hundred in
1970 and, no doubt, have increased greatly in the last six
years. Forty-four Masons have places of high honor in the
Baseball Hall of Fame at Cooperstown, New York. Among
them are Ty Cobb, Bob Feller and Christy Mathewson. Of
special note is Brother Earle Bryan Combs. He has celebrated more than fifty years as a Mason and was elected to
the Cooperstown Hall of Fame due to his record while
playing for the New York Yankees from 1924 to 1936. He
played 1,454 games and had a lifetime batting average of
.325. After 1936 he coached for the Yankees, the St. Louis
Browns, Boston Red Sox and Philadelphia Phillies.

Whether in music, theatre, film, radio, television or ath-
letics, Freemasons have attained national positions and
held the attention of America through their art and ability.
Their relationship to Freemasonry encouraged their
achievements as symbolic of what man can attain when
inspired with high ideals and beneficial goals. Their fame
as artists and athletes also gave credit to the Craft in mak-

ing millions of Americans aware of Freemasonry as one of the chief pillars of American society. They came to recognize the relationship between Masonry and character, between aspiration and success, between patriotism and service. Men who had never heard previously of Freemasonry saw its results in these great Americans and often were brought to the threshold of their local Lodge by the example of these outstanding Brethren.

America owes much to Freemasonry. Freemasons owe much to America. The relationship is mutual and beneficial. The bounty of the land allowed opportunity, and members of the Craft were quick to take the offered gift. The principles of Freemasonry had taught them to explore and develop, not to exploit and destroy. They returned to the land and to the society it supported greater benefits than the material and human resources they had utilized. At the end of their labors, these outstanding American Freemasons, who are representative of all the Brethren that work diligently to fulfill Masonic goals, left America not poorer but richer in wealth and spirit. They gave of themselves.

Thus they began the act of creation that has been continuous for these two hundred years celebrated up to our Bicentennial Year, 1976. The creation is still going on. America is growing and becoming greater every day and we, as individual Freemasons and as a Fraternity, have been and are an essential part of that creative process. We make it happen. Let us continue the example of yesterday through action today. Let us carry on the tradition of Freemasonry that has made America the greatest Nation in the world. It is our duty. It is our glory. Truly, patriotism, freedom and accomplishment are the touchstones of Freemasonry. We accept this three-fold heritage of our country and our Craft. It is ours to preserve—we must and we shall.

OUR LEGACY:
A Source of Freedom and Justice For All

It is fitting, after glancing at the creative process of the birth and growth of our Nation and the great contributions of Freemasons to America, that we should return to where we, as a people, began—to that most fundamental and innovative of eras in our national history, the Revolution. During this period of foundation-building, Freemasonry put its indelible stamp upon America. Since then, our Nation has developed as an extension and continuation of that pattern. The old adage, "As the twig is bent, so the tree shall grow," is appropriate here. From the "twig" of an infant Republic struggling for freedom and independence in a world that huge colonial powers then dominated, America has grown today into a mighty "tree of liberty," bearing abundantly and for all. Our legacy—a source of freedom and justice for all—started to take shape and form two centuries ago. It is to the Fraternity's eternal pride and honor that the leaders and majority of these Architects of Freedom were Masons.

What bravery must have been required, what perseverance and dedication to principle were necessary in that ordeal that led to the Declaration of Independence! The British Navigation Acts, The Sugar Act and The Stamp Act were, as James Otis asserted, direct violations of the rights of colonists "as British subjects *and* men." American resentment grew. The English Parliament ignored its own heritage of freedom and attempted to impose tyranny upon America. But the colonials had not forgotten freedom. Many had learned of it from another source— Freemasonry. In reaction to "The Boston Massacre" and in participation with The Committees of Correspondence, in the First and Second Continental Congresses, in the Boston Tea Party, and in the battles of Lexington, Concord and Bunker's Hill, Freemasons turned their Masonic dedication to liberty into acts of liberty. They would be bound no more. The Craft had taught them the inherent dignity of man under God. Americans would be free men—or die.

Certainly the possibility of failure was evident in that hot July of 1776 when delegates from each of the Thirteen Colonies resolved and passed the Declaration of Independence. Each signer risked his position, property and life itself. Yet, they had faith in America, its people, and in God, and they were willing to pledge to independence their lives, fortunes and sacred honor. In ringing words they declared the creation of a new nation under God:

> We, therefore, the Representatives of the United States of America, in General Congress, Assembled, appealing to the Supreme Judge of the world for the rectitude of our intentions, do, in the Name, and by Authority of the good People of these Colonies, solemnly publish and declare, That these United Colonies are, and of Right ought to be, Free and Independent States.

Of the 56 patriots who finally signed this immortal document establishing America, a goodly number were Freemasons, which indicates the contribution of the Craft to the formation of America. Our Brethren not only were among the willing signers of the Declaration of Independence, but they continued to lead in the Revolution that followed. General George Washington, the foremost of Americans and Freemasons, as Commander-in-Chief of the Army, saw us through the perilous war years, and, as President, through the first eight years of our existence as a nation under the Constitution. Assisting Brother

Washington in his purpose were fellow Freemasons in every level of the Army and Government from the humblest foot soldiers to the highest statesman. These dedicated Brethren changed an ideal and assertion of freedom into a fact. In the Peace of Paris, that Brother Benjamin Franklin negotiated in 1783, America formally assumed a position in the world community as a free and independent nation.

Though free, we were not yet united. The loose Articles of Confederation did not provide a strong national government, common currency or consistent judicial system. Men of vision realized that another step must be taken if the weak Confederation of American States was to become a strong, unified nation. Again Freemasonry set the pattern in ideology and form. Since the Masonic federal system of organization was the only pattern for effective organization operating in each of the original Thirteen Colonies, it was natural that patriotic Brethren intent on strengthening the fledgling nation should turn to the organizational base of the Craft for a model. Regardless of the other forces that affected the formation of the Constitution during the Constitutional Convention in 1787, the fact remains that the federalism established in the civil government the Constitution created is identical to the federalism of the Grand Lodge system of Masonic government created in *Anderson's Constitutions* of 1723.

In purpose as well as in form, the Constitution reflects Masonic influence. Freedom, justice, equity and fraternity are the four cornerstones of the symbolic Temple of Freemasonry, and the Constitution reveals these ideals in many phrases. This may well be due to the fact the President of the Constitutional Convention, General George Washington and its leaders were Freemasons. Perhaps the most famous and respected delegate, Benjamin Franklin, back from France where he greatly helped the Revolution through winning foreign support, was an ardent Freema-

H. Armstrong Roberts—Philadelphia, Pennsylvania

son. In all, 23 of the 39 patriots who signed the Constitution were Brothers in the Craft. As participants in the signing of the Declaration of Independence, Freemasons had declared America independent and set the American people on the path to full nationhood. Now, in the formation of the Constitution, a majority of signers were Freemasons. They consolidated into a single statement, the Constitution, the freedom won over a decade of fighting as "the greatest document ever struck off by the brain and purpose of man." Today it is the longest lasting, continuously in effect constitution of any nation in the world. The Constitution is as strong today as it was when ratified in 1789, because generations of Americans and, in particular, Freemasons, have struggled to defend it as the Supreme Law of the Land.

The Supreme Court of the United States has been in the front ranks of this defense. As of recent date, 35 of the 96 Justices of The Supreme Court have been Freemasons. This tradition began when President Washington appointed the first Justices, the court then numbered six, and two of these—William Cushing of Massachusetts and John Blair of Virginia—were Freemasons. Brother Cushing, in the absence of John Jay, acted as Chief Justice, and he administered the oath of office to Brother Washington at his second inauguration. During his two terms in office, President Washington appointed two more Brethren to the highest court in the land—William Paterson of New Jersey and Oliver Ellsworth of Connecticut. Therefore, a majority of those that Washington appointed during this crucial early period of the court were Freemasons!

The greatest jurist in American history was Chief Justice John Marshall, whose influence is permanent. A member of Richmond Lodge No. 13 (now No. 10) of Richmond, Virginia, Brother Marshall took the concept of judicial review stated in the Constitution and fashioned it into a fact and precedent, thus making The Supreme Court the place of last resort above local, State and Federal laws and, so, truly "Supreme." Under Brother Marshall as Chief Justice from 1801 to 1835, The Supreme Court became a symbol of national unity, the absolute arbiter of constitutionality, and an effective counterbalance to the Legislative and Executive Branches of the government. Tradition has it that in 1835 when Brother Marshall died, the Liberty Bell in Philadelphia, which had proclaimed "liberty throughout all the land unto all the inhabitants thereof," was cracked and stilled after ringing out the death of one of liberty's greatest exponents and defenders.

The record of achievement of the other Brethren who served on The Supreme Court is too long and illustrious to detail here, but at least Justice Robert H. Jackson and Chief Justices William Howard Taft and Earl Warren should be noted. While serving on the Court, Justice Jackson was asked by President Truman to serve as the United States Prosecutor at the Nuremberg war crimes trials of high-ranking Nazi officials. In this difficult and epochal role, Justice Jackson brought his Masonic and American ideals of justice to the attention of the world. He underlined the fact that concepts of moral conduct are universal and that violations of human brotherhood are heinous crimes in any time or place. Brother William Howard Taft, after a distinguished term as President, became Chief Justice of the United States in 1921 and so was the only man in American history to serve as both President and Chief Justice—the highest elective and appointive offices of the United States Government. Earl Warren, who served as Chief Justice from 1953 to 1969, was a Past Grand Master of the Grand Lodge of California and a Thirty-third Degree member of the Scottish Rite.

Words, ultimately, cannot do justice to the contributions of Freemasonry to America. Simple facts of name, place, date and act are insufficient to capture the spirit and labor behind the historical record. Even such monumental attempts as Brother Gutzon Borglum's awe-inspiring sculpture at Mount Rushmore are insufficient to represent the greatness of America and of Freemasonry. This Past Master of Howard Lodge No. 35, New York City, carved the world's largest monument out of living rock. It depicts two Freemasons—George Washington and Theodore Roosevelt. Jefferson and Lincoln are said to have been Masonic minded. Millions every year visit this patriotic shrine for it, like the Declaration of Independence, the Constitution and the Bill of Rights, clearly springs from the spirit and teachings of Freemasonry. Like Brother Borglum, the men who labored to create, interpret and sustain these documents were Freemasons. They set the pattern for a free, progressive American nation that other Freemasons fulfilled in the areas of exploration, government, the military, industry, science and entertainment. Spirtual leaders like Brothers Daniel Alfred Poling and Norman Vincent Peale, 33°, in turn, supported them. No other private and charitable organization has contributed more to the greatness of America than the Masonic Fraternity. In inspiration and in action, the Craft has led men to enlightenment and urged them to make their Masonic ideals come alive.

Patriotism. Freedom. Accomplishment. This brief glance at our Masonic heritage in America began, appropriately, with these three significant words. Patriotism is not an outdated word to a Freemason. It is, rather, the inner motivating principle of his life, as it was for those great men who formed our national legacy in the Declaration of Independence, the Constitution and Bill of Rights. Above all else, men like George Washington and Benjamin Franklin were patriots serving the Nation. A Freemason today, as throughout American history, is also a patriot, a man who

H. Armstrong Roberts—Philadelphia, Pennsylvania

loves his country and seeks to serve humanity. The guiding beacon of his life in this endeavor is the ideal of Freedom.

Freedom to speak and write, freedom to vote or campaign, and, most of all, freedom to work and worship— these are among our basic freedoms given to us by men of vision two hundred years ago and that Freemasons have sustained ever since. From these freedoms springs opportunity and individual enterprise. All who are willing to try can have opportunities to succeed. The Masonic defense of American Individualism and the Free Enterprise System based on honest endeavor, thrift, work and self-development allows each American an equal chance to improve himself and his country. Infringements on this basic liberty and encroachments on individualism from whatever sector are contrary to Freemasonry's ideal of Freedom, an ideal that fellow Freemasons made the basic structure of our founding documents. Freedom is written as boldly in the text of the Constitution as Brother John Hancock's outsized signature is placed on the Declaration of Independence. Freedom has been our means and greater freedom our goal. Let us ever recall this sacred heritage.

Finally, accomplishment is the product of the Masonic principles of Patriotism and Freedom. The few acts of achievement recorded here are but the leading edge of Freemasonry's contribution to America. The record is too vast, the cast too numerous, and the scope too broad to trace in more than general outline in this brief survey, but the point is clear. Freemasons helped conceive and build and shape this Nation. The concept of the Brotherhood of Man under the Fatherhood of God resulted in practical works for every area of American life and in every era of American history. Our task now is to sustain and extend what others have created. The charge is not to tear down and build again. The foundation is firm, the structure is sturdy. We can best serve our Nation and our Fraternity in this Bicentennial Year of 1976 if we remember with pride the history and character of American Freemasonry. With this as inspiration and model, our path is clear and our faith is firm. Let us serve America as so many thousands of Brethren before us have served. Then, we, too, will win the gratitude and glory of American generations yet to come.

Washington Addressing the Constitutional Convention
Courtesy Virginia Museum of Fine Arts, Richmond, Virginia

DEUS MEUMQUE JUS.

The cause of human progress is our cause, the enfranchisement of human thought our supreme wish, the freedom of human conscience our mission, and the guarantee of equal rights to all peoples everywhere, the end of our contention.

James D. Richardson. 33°

Sov.·. Grand Commander.

SALUTE TO THE SCOTTISH RITE

What *is* the Scottish Rite of Freemasonry? This is a difficult question to answer and may best be approached by pointing out what it is *not*. It is not the formal organization. Nor is it our magnificent temples. Nor is it a severely secret society. Nor is it merely ritual. Perhaps we should content ourselves with the fundamental definition of Masonry as "a peculiar system of morality, veiled in allegory, and illustrated by symbols."

Historically, the Scottish Rite of Freemasonry as we know it evolved over 200 years ago on the Continent of Europe as the Rite of Perfection under the Constitutions and Regulations of 1762. Later, the Grand Constitutions of 1786 were enacted and this combined base became the creative laws for us and all our descendant Supreme Councils of the Ancient and Accepted Scottish Rite.

"Established on the 31st of May, 1801, at Charleston," states our own illustrious Albert Pike in his *Allocution* of 1876, The Supreme Council "appears to have at first consisted of the Count Alexandre Francois August de Grasse-Tilly, his father-in-law, Jean Baptiste Marie de la Hogue, Colonel John Mitchell, and Dr. Frederick Dalcho. The Patent of the Ill.·.Bro.·.de Grasse bears date the 21st day of February, 1802, declares him to be Sovereign Grand Inspector General, and Member of the Supreme Council, and also Grand Commander for life in the French West Indian Islands; and it is signed by Colonel John Mitchell, as

Grand Commander, Dr. Frederick Dalcho, as Lieut.∴ Grand Commander, Dr. Isaac Auld, Thomas Bartholomew Bowen, Jean Baptiste Marie de la Hogue, as Sov.∴G.∴ Inspector General, and Lieut.∴.Gr.∴Commander of the French West Indies, Israel de Lieben, and Abraham Alexander. Emanuel de la Motta was also a member, as early as July 5th, 1801; and the venerable Moses C. Levy and Dr. James Moultrie had become so before the 4th of December, 1802.

"By the 12th of February, 1802, the Ill.∴Bro.∴de Grasse had established at Cap Francais, in the Island of Haiti, a Supreme Council for the Windward and Leeward West Indian Islands, of which he was Grand Commander, and the Ill.∴Bro.∴de la Hogue, Lieut.∴Gr.∴Commander; both having retired from The Supreme Council of the United States, so soon, it appears, as three members besides themselves composed it.

"Colonel John Mitchell was a Justice and Notary, then 60 years of age, a native of Ireland, late Lieutenant Colonel in the American Army, and a member of the Society of the Cincinnati.

"Dr. Dalcho, 32 years of age, was a native of England, an Episcopalian.

"Dr. Isaac Auld, 32 years of age, was a native of Pennsylvania, a Presbyterian.

"Thomas Bartholomew Bowen, a printer, 60 years of age, had been a Major in the American Army, and was a member of the Cincinnati.

"Israel de Lieben, a commission merchant, 61 years of age, was a native of Bohemia.

"Emanuel de la Motta, commission merchant and auctioneer, 42 years of age, was a native of the Island of Santa Cruz.

"Abraham Alexander was, it is believed, a native of South Carolina.

"Moses C. Levy was born at Cracow, in Poland.

"Dr. James Moultrie, 33 years of age, was a native of South Carolina.

"And the Ill.·.Brethren de Lieben, Levy, and De la Motta, were Hebrews, of the ancient and pure faith of the children of Israel.

"Such were the men, of whose lives we would fain know more, who were the first Members of 'The Supreme Council of the United States,' mother of every legitimate Supreme Council in the World."

The line of Sovereign Grand Commanders in the Mother Jurisdiction is continuous and unbroken from the beginning. John Mitchell held the office from 1801 to 1816; Frederick Dalcho, from 1816 to 1822; Isaac Auld, from 1822 to 1826; Moses Holbrook, from 1826 to 1844; Alexander McDonald, from 1844 to 1846; John Henry Honour, from 1846 to 1859; Albert Pike, from 1859 to 1891; James C. Batchelor, from, 1891 to 1893; Philip C. Tucker, from 1893 to 1894; Thomas H. Caswell, from 1894 to 1900; James D. Richardson, from 1901 to 1914; George F. Moore, from 1914 to 1921; John H. Cowles, from 1921 to 1952; Thomas J. Harkins, from 1952 to 1955; Luther A. Smith, from 1955 to 1969; and, since October 1969, your present Grand Commander, Henry C. Clausen.

The Charleston, South Carolina-based Southern Jurisdiction of the Scottish Rite is the Mother Supreme Council of the World. Therefore, all educational, religious, patriotic and charitable activities of the Order may be said to have had their genesis in this founding organization.

The rich heritage thus handed down across the generations of 175 years spans also the developing years of our Nation. It charges us with awe-inspiring obligations. Your Supreme Council and your present Sovereign Grand Commander are dedicated to sustaining and applying

John Mitchell

Frederick Dalcho

Isaac Auld

Henry Christian Clausen

Moses Holbrook

Alexander McDonald

Luther Andrew Smith

Johny Henry Honour

Thomas Joshua Harkins

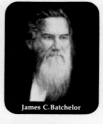
Albert Pike

John Henry Cowles

The ''Birthplace'' of The Supreme Council,
corner of Church and Broad Streets,
Charleston, South Carolina.

James C. Batchelor

George Fleming Moore

James Daniel Richardson

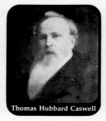
Thomas Hubbard Caswell

Phillip Crosby Tucker

those obligations to ever greater tasks.

Freemasonry has accomplished much in every field of American life, and the evidence of our achievement is both spiritual and physical. Spiritually, Freemasons have applied to their everyday civic, commercial and domestic lives the Craft's ideals of Freedom, Equity, Courage and Patriotism. They have built personal character and community, state and national strength.

Physically, too, the Scottish Rite has erected edifices that testify to the ideals of Freemasonry. A visitor entering the monumental House of the Temple of The Supreme Council, 33°, Mother Council of the World, on Sixteenth Street in the Nation's Capital—the nerve center of our executive, administrative and evangelistic endeavors—might never realize that the potential this structure reflects has channeled millions of dollars into our educational and charitable concerns, including the rehabilitation of afflicted children. The domed Temple Room, where the ceiling soars 88 feet above the floor, symbolizes the heights and the aims to which our members aspire.

The Supreme Council devotes large sums to education. We seek to inculcate the ideals of Freemasonry and of Americanism into local, state and national affairs. Scottish Rite Masonry strives to preserve the fundamentals and principles of the American Government, to protect moral values and to develop America spiritually.

On a practical humanitarian level, we help in the training and healing of children suffering aphasic and learning disorders and orthopedic handicaps. The results have been gratifying undertakings to which a number of Orients have pioneered and contributed generously.

For the first 115 years of its existence, from 1801 to 1914, The Supreme Council probably exerted its greatest and most inspirational strength in motivating our own members to practice the noble purposes of Freemasonry in their

Present day
House of the Temple

Pike's
House of the Temple

Shepherd's Tavern

The three buildings in which the Mother Jurisdiction has been housed

individual lives. Because members of the Scottish Rite have always held influential positions in business, in the professions, and in government, this character development had a great beneficial impact upon American life.

With the dedication of the House of the Temple in 1915, The Supreme Council began to expand its activities, making the immediate past 60 years of perhaps even greater value to the Nation than the first 115 years had been.

HISTORICAL PROJECTS

Before describing the larger, far-reaching programs of The Supreme Council, it is fitting, in this Bicentennial Year of our Nation, to mention two historical projects of which the membership is justly proud:

A statue of George Washington, The Supreme Council commissioned and financed, stands in a bay of the National Cathedral at Washington, D.C. The Cathedral is, of course, a national symbol of religious faith for the entire Nation.

The statue, slightly larger than life size, was dedicated in 1965. Sculptor Lee Laurie carved this from Vermont marble, and it honors George Washington's support of Masonic principles in his great service to our country. On the pedestal are inscribed these words: "George Washington, First Citizen, Churchman, President, Statesman, Farmer, Soldier, Patriot, Freemason."

A Scottish Rite museum of Washington memorabilia, which our Supreme Council installed, occupies the fourth floor of The George Washington Masonic National Memorial in Alexandria, Virginia. This imposing room was sponsored jointly with the Northern Masonic Jurisdiction, each paying $45,000 toward the cost. It is reported that since it was opened ten years ago, a million visitors have seen the fine collection in this handsome room. The museum is proud to have many mementos of our First President, including the Washington family Bible.

The George Washington Museum was the gift of the Supreme Councils of the Scottish Rite for the Southern and Northern Jurisdictions.

Statue of George Washington
at the National Cathedral in Washington, D.C.

EDUCATIONAL ACTIVITIES

The single largest cash grant The Supreme Council made for education was the gift of one million dollars in 1927 to The George Washington University in the Nation's Capital to endow a School of Government. This school was established to teach "constitutional government in the light of American traditions."

The School of Government was established in accord with a wish expressed by George Washington himself, the great leader for whom the University is named. He said it was his desire that a school should be set up in the city to give young Americans a knowledge of government. Areas of study in the present school cover international and national affairs, public administration, personnel administration, and Sino-Soviet and Far Eastern Studies.

In further support of the School of Government, the Scottish Rite now gives annual fellowships to young men and women who meet necessary entrance requirements, each for one year of graduate study. More than 400 young men and women have completed a year of such study as Scottish Rite Fellows. Many of these are now employed in foreign service, in government at state and national levels, in universities throughout the world, and in private business or in the professions.

Other Educational Grants

The Supreme Council does not limit its educational grants to one university. Other gifts have been made to many worthwhile educational institutions including Baylor University; American University; Doane College of Crete, Nebraska; College of the Pacific (now University of the Pacific); Leland Stanford, Jr., University; Uta Halee Home for Girls; West Central 4-H Educational Center;

The Hall of Government at The George Washington University

Foundation for Economic Education; and Americans United Research Foundation.

The Supreme Council has strong convictions that we should preserve the traditional American system of separation of church and state. Lectures, organized research, and well-planned courses for college credit, among other things, are all included in an effort to maintain intact Jefferson's Wall of Separation—the complete separation of denominational institutions from State and Federal financial support and entanglements.

Education on every level of American life is of interest to

Freemasonry, and support of the public schools in our Nation is a matter of vital concern to The Supreme Council. For each of the past ten years, The Supreme Council has awarded annually two scholarships to experienced public school teachers and administrators who wish to study for doctoral degrees in public school administration. These scholarships are now for $10,000 each, given at the rate of $5,000 a year for two years of this advanced graduate study.

PRINTED PUBLICATIONS

Knowing the power of the printed word, The Supreme Council has issued over a period of years—along with Rituals, dissertations on philosophies and religions of the past, histories, Pike's *Bulletins* and his *Morals and Dogma*, *Clausen's Commentaries on Morals and Dogma*, and *The New Age* Magazine—educational booklets for distribution to schools and interested individuals all over the Nation.

Newest of the educational booklets is a series of four under the group title, *Dynamic Freedoms.*

Our Freedom Documents was the first of the Dynamic Freedoms series to be issued. It contains not only the Declaration of Independence and the Constitution of the United States, but also one of the Federalist Papers of colonial days, whose sound arguments helped persuade the American Colonies to adopt the Constitution under which we are governed.

Also included in this booklet is the Mayflower Compact, a simple statement that governed Plymouth for ten years, and which later became the basis of similar government for the entire Massachusetts Colony.

Communism–Enemy of All Freedoms is the second booklet. This publication outlines the specific means by which communist nations work unceasingly for world domination.

Separation of Church and State is the third title in the Dynamic Freedoms series. This outlines the dangers and disastrous results that would occur through loss of religious freedom in the United States if at any time our government should deviate from the traditional principle that civil law and administration should not intrude into our individual faith or upon church beliefs. It also points out why State or Federal aid should not be entangled with denominational institutions.

Free Enterprise–An American Invention is the arresting title of the final booklet of the series. This explains the system which has brought the people of our Nation to the highest standard of living in the world.

Preceding the Dynamic Freedoms series, The Supreme Council issued seven booklets on the various aspects of the American constitutional system. This material was first published, one subject at a time, each as a special issue of *The New Age*, official publication of The Supreme Council. Eight million copies of these booklets were distributed to private schools, to libraries, and to individuals.

Outstanding speeches by patriotic Americans have also been printed in large numbers for wide distribution. The aim of all the inspirational material, is "to make better men in a better world, happier men in a happier world, and wiser men in a wiser world," as an official purpose of The Supreme Council.

FILMS

Three films produced before 1970, and one issued in 1974, have had excellent acceptance. One of these, "Summer of Decision," received this comment from a critic, "Every student in every public school, every member of the Armed Forces, and, in fact, every citizen in America should see this film."

"The Supreme Council in Action" is the newest film. It is a handsome picture story of The Supreme Council and the House of the Temple.

SCOTTISH RITE HOSPITALS

In 1915, the year The Supreme Council dedicated the House of the Temple, the first Scottish Rite Hospital for Crippled Children was opened. This was at Decatur, Georgia, under sponsorship of the Georgia Orient of the Scottish Rite. It was the first hospital of that kind the Scottish Rite Masons established and was the pattern for the chain of similar hospitals of the Shrine.

With only twenty beds at first, the Decatur hospital soon became so well known, and the demand for its services so great, that a new building for 48 patients was constructed only four years after the original opening. Care and treatment at a total cost of more than $25,000,000 has been given to 23,000 young patients in the sixty-one years of the hospital's operation. This year a new modern hospital in Atlanta, Georgia, will replace the one at Decatur.

Dallas, Texas, is the site of another Scottish Rite Hospital for crippled children. Masons and organizations in Texas provide approximately $2,500,000 each year to maintain these facilities. Five buildings have been built on the seven-acre hospital grounds, with a 78-bed capacity. A single large building with 100 beds is expected to be completed soon to replace the former facilities. In its more than half a century of existence, this hospital has cared for 200,000 young boys and girls.

Children are admitted to the Dallas and Atlanta hospitals

The Scottish Rite Hospital for
Crippled Children in Atlanta, Georgia

The Scottish Rite Hospital for
Crippled Children in Dallas, Texas

without regard for race, color or creed. The child must be below 15 years of age, must have a handicap which promises to be curable, and must come from a family unable to pay for private hospital care.

Treatment for Aphasia

Children suffering from aphasia afflictions have aroused the compassion of Scottish Rite members in many States. These children have serious difficulty in learning to speak. Closely related brain malfunctions result in similar inability to read, write and communicate in other ways.

The California Scottish Rite Foundation in 1958 established the Scottish Rite Institute for Childhood Aphasia at the School of Medicine in Stanford University. In 1973 this project was moved to San Francisco State University. More than 3,500 children have been helped in the clinics in addition to research on the subject. A large number of professional workers in speech and language therapy and related fields also have received training there for service elsewhere throughout the Nation. Several other centers for remedial help to aphasic children have also been opened in California.

Colorado Scottish Rite members opened their work for brain-injured aphasic children in 1952. The Children's Hospital at Denver is the service center of this undertaking. More than 700 children have been treated for periods ranging from one year to three years, and many have been substantially cured.

The newest project for aphasic children was started in Oklahoma. Located at Phillips University in Enid, the new center is supported by Scottish Rite members from Tulsa, McAlester and Guthrie.

Other States taking up this worthwhile mission of healing and training, as of this date, are Florida, Kansas, Mississippi, North Carolina, Tennessee and Virginia.

SUPREME COUNCIL FOUNDATION

In order to better unify and organize the educational and charitable activities of The Supreme Council, the Scottish Rite Foundation, Southern Jurisdiction, U.S.A., Inc., was established in 1954. In a generous and far-sighted move, The Supreme Council immediately assumed all administrative expenses of the Foundation, so that every dollar received from bequest or through outright gifts will go entirely for the worthwhile objectives intended.

Under its charter, the Foundation may support not only charitable and educational purposes, but may also assist scientific, religious and literary projects. All gifts and bequests to the foundation are deductible under State and Federal income tax laws, and are also exempt from Federal estate and State inheritance taxes.

LIBRARY, ARCHIVES AND ROBERT BURNS COLLECTION

A priceless treasure of The Supreme Council is its Library. One-third of the 175,000 volumes which it contains deal with Freemasonry in all its branches, forming one of the most comprehensive collections on this subject in the entire world.

The Supreme Council has the honor of having established this in 1888 in the District of Columbia as the first library open for free public use. Albert Pike, then Sovereign Grand Commander, had previously presented his private library to The Supreme Council. More books were added, and when the collection had grown to 8,000 volumes, he directed that the books should be made available to all citizens.

The Archives in the House of the Temple supplement the Library. More than two-and-a-half million papers, giving details of the history of Masonry and of the Scottish Rite are carefully filed and indexed. These materials are open to any interested researcher, and hundreds of Brethren have found the Archives a fruitful source for examination of primary documents and rare materials.

Robert Burns, the beloved Scottish poet and loyal Freemason, is honored in the Burnsiana Room. This is the world's richest storehouse of Burns memorabilia and writings outside of Scotland. William Smith assembled the collection. He was director of the Botanic Gardens in Washington, D.C. The material was placed in the House of the Temple at the suggestion of Andrew Carnegie, trustee of Mr. Smith's estate.

CONCLUSION

The preceding spotlight of a 175 years survey of the origin, development and present accomplishments of The Supreme Council does not do justice, of course, to the complex history and varied achievements of this great Masonic organization. Programs, publications, films, foundations, hospitals, libraries, archives—these are simply some of the categories of endeavor in which thousands upon thousands of Brethren have united in cooperative spirit and intense dedication. The real success and enterprise of The Supreme Council and the Brethren during these 175 years is unseen and unrecorded. It is made up of enlightened minds, of strengthened characters, and of an American people bettered in moral health, patriotic education and spiritual aspirations.

This, ultimately, is the core of Freemasonry, an ideal "system of morality, veiled in allegory, and illustrated by symbols." It is understandable to all men, for the allegorical and symbolic aspects do not obscure but rather clarify and elevate each individual's conception, allowing him to transcend his isolation and, instead, join with his fellow men as a spiritual brother. Scottish Rite Freemasonry, then, draws men together, improves them, and leads them in a fulfillment and enrichment of their lives through altruistic and humanitarian service. It is a positive, optimistic, forward-looking philosophy that is not content merely to extoll the past. On the contrary, Scottish Rite Freemasonry looks to the future, assured that past and present accomplishments are merely the basis for greater work tomorrow. We may be proud of our Scottish Rite history, as set forth in this brief survey, but our greatest satisfaction is to know that the future opens ever wider horizons for our endeavors. Thus, the devoted Brethren who are the very heart and soul of American Freemasonry say, "All hail to a great past and to an even greater future!"

The purpose of the Scottish Rite, simply stated, is to seek that which is the most worth in the world; to exalt the dignity of every person, the human side of our daily activities, and the maximum service to humanity; to aid mankind's search in God's universe for identity, for development and for destiny, and thereby achieve better men in a better world, happier men in a happier world and wiser men in a wiser world.

Sovereign Grand Commander